UNITE History
Volume 6 (1992–2010)

The Transport and General Workers' Union (TGWU):
Unity for a New Era

UNITE History
Volume 6
(1992–2010)

The Transport & General Workers' Union: Unity for a New Era

Adrian Weir

LIVERPOOL UNIVERSITY PRESS

In memory of Pat Hayes, Les Ford,
Chris Russell and Mike Hayes

First published 2023 by
Liverpool University Press
4 Cambridge Street
Liverpool
L69 7ZU

British Library Cataloguing-in-Publication data
A British Library CIP record is available

ISBN 978-1-80207-486-4

Typeset by Carnegie Book Production, Lancaster
Printed and bound by CPI Group (UK) Ltd, Croydon CR0 4YY

Contents

Figures

Tables

Boxes

Acknowledgements

This volume is the last in a series of six commissioned by Unite to mark the centenary of the foundation of the Transport & General Workers' Union (T&G) in 1922. Thanks are due to Len McCluskey, former General Secretary of Unite, and Andrew Murray, former Chief of Staff at Unite, for initiating the project. Thanks also to Sharon Graham, current Unite General Secretary, for seeing the project through to conclusion.

This book has had an unusual genesis to say the least. This volume was originally allocated to the former T&G National Organiser, the late Graham Stevenson, to write but Graham sadly died with only an outline written. The task of completing the work then fell to me. At that time I was Assistant Chief of Staff at Unite, now retired.

I am especially grateful to members of the Unite History Project writing team organised by the Marx Memorial Library – Professors Mary Davis, John Foster and Marjorie Mayo – for their tremendous assistance with either writing or co-writing sections of this volume. Marj for co-writing Chapter 3, Mary for Chapter 4 on equalities and John for the work on devolution in Scotland and the north of Ireland in Chapter 5.

Thanks also to Dr John Fisher, retired T&G Director of Research & Education, for writing the section on Total Quality Management in Chapter 2 and Keith Jones, retired T&G Regional Education Officer, for initial ideas on the politics of Welsh devolution covered in Chapter 5. Thanks to recently retired Unite Assistant General Secretary Diana Holland who was generous with her time and allowed access to her equalities archive.

I am grateful to Natasha Hickman, Communications Officer at Cuba Solidarity Campaign, for her assistance in setting out the chronology of the T&G's involvement with the Miami 5 campaign and for correcting my not always accurate recollections.

Thanks to Meirian Jump, Archivist & Library Manager at the Marx Memorial Library, who has provided the secretariat for the entire project in liaison with Jim Mowatt, formerly Unite Director of Education.

A great number of people were generous with their time by agreeing to be interviewed by members of the writing team: Len McCluskey, Andrew Murray, Barry Camfield, Tony Burke, Chris Kaufman, Tony Gould, Dave Turnbull, Miles Hubbard, Ivan Crane, Andy Green, Sam Gurney, Orlando Martins, Teresa Mackay, Barry Salmon, Joe Bowers, Peter Bunting, Kevin Cooper, Maurice Cunningham, Eugene McGlone, Mick O'Reilly, Jackson Cullinane, Jane McKay, Dave Moxam, Yvonne Strachan and Pat Stuart.

I have used the abbreviation T&G throughout; earlier volumes mainly used TGWU; my choice of T&G is because this volume more or less starts during the period when the union commissioned Klein & Co, US management consultants with alleged links to the US labour movement, to conduct a root and branch review of the union and its operations. A point picked up by Klein was that the union had 11 regions and the head office all using different branding. Klein & Co's report *One Union, T&G* led to unified branding and the accepted use of T&G as the union's public name.

Abbreviations

ACTU	Australian Council of Trade Unions
AEEU	Amalgamated Engineering & Electrical Union
AFL-CIO	American Federation of Labor–Congress of Industrial Organisations
ASLEF	Associated Society of Locomotive Engineers and Firemen
ATGWU	Amalgamated Transport & General Workers Union (the Irish section of the T&G)
BA	British Airways
BAEM	Black, Asian and Ethnic Minority
BALPA	British Airline Pilots' Association
BASSA	British Airlines Stewards & Stewardesses Association (a branch of T&G/Unite)
BDC	Biennial Delegates' Conference (of the T&G)
BEA	British European Airways
BOAC	British Overseas Airways Corporation
CLP	Constituency Labour Party
CSC	Cuba Solidarity Campaign
EPIU	Electrical & Plumbing Industries Union
EPLP	European Parliamentary Labour Party
EU	European Union
FBU	Fire Brigades Union
FTAT	Furniture, Timber and Allied Trades Union
GCHQ	Government Communications Headquarters
GEC	General Executive Council (of the T&G)
GLC	Greater London Council
GLEB	Greater London Enterprise Board
GMB	General, Municipal and Boilermakers Union
GPMU	Graphical, Paper & Media Union
GUF	global union federation
HRM	human resources management
ICTU	Irish Congress of Trades Unions

IDC	International Dockworkers' Council
ITF	International Transport Workers' Federation
ITS	international trade secretariat
LGBT	lesbian, gay, bisexual and transgender
MDHC	Mersey Docks & Harbour Company
MSF	Manufacturing, Science & Finance Union
NATFHE	National Association of Teachers in Further & Higher Education
NDLB	National Dock Labour Board
NGA	National Graphical Association
NHS	National Health Service
NIC ICTU	Northern Ireland Committee of the ICTU
NUJ	National Union of Journalists
NUM	National Union of Mineworkers
NUR	National Union of Railwaymen
NUS	National Union of Seamen
NWAC	National Women's Advisory Committee
ODA	Olympic Delivery Authority
OMOV	one member, one vote
PCS	Public & Commercial Services Union
PFI	private finance initiative
PLP	Parliamentary Labour Party
QWL	quality of working life
REC	Race Equality Committee
RMT	National Union of Rail, Maritime & Transport Workers
RREC	Regional Race Equality Committee
RWAC	Regional Women's Advisory Committee
SEEDA	South East England Development Agency
SEIU	Service Employees International Union
SERTUC	South East Region of the TUC
STE	Society of Telecom Executives
STUC	Scottish Trades Union Congress
T&G	Transport & General Workers' Union
TfL	Transport for London
TQM	total quality management
TUC	Trades Union Congress
TUFL	Trade Unions for Labour
UCATT	Union of Construction, Allied Trades and Technicians
UCU	University and College Union
USDAW	Union of Shop, Distributive & Allied Workers
WLP	Welsh Labour Party
WLP EC	Welsh Labour Party Executive Committee
WR&E	Women, Race and Equalities

Foreword

Unite History Project
The Six-Volume History

2022 marked the centenary of the formation of the Transport & General Workers' Union (T&G), now a part of Unite, Britain and Ireland's largest union in private industry. The T&G was also a significant workers' organisation in public sector employment; a tradition carried forward into Unite.

The T&G was the first general trade union. It exercised a dominant influence within the Labour Party in Britain through the twentieth century. This and its interaction with government provides the basis for a wider chronological history of the Labour Movement in Britain – and to that extent also the political history of Britain and not without a significant impact in Ireland as well.

This history reflects and exposes the wider processes of social change in which union members played an active role – in terms of an understanding of oppression in society and exploitation in the workplace, particularly of women and Black people. In addition, the union's international work and campaigns are brought into sharp focus.

Many of the T&G's general secretaries, from Bevin to Morris, have been the subject of biographies and Jack Jones published an autobiography; but this series is different. Among other things it examines how the union's central function, campaigning and winning on jobs, pay and conditions, evolved over the course of the twentieth century.

This six-volume series tells this story in a highly original way, as it enables the incorporation of local history as played out by the union's shop stewards and branch officers. Work has been undertaken at regional level based on interviews and newly uncovered archival material that brings *our* history to life and gives a human dimension to an otherwise 'top-level' narrative. Unions are, after all, composed of individuals – in the T&G's case of hundreds of thousands.

I believe that these volumes will make a great contribution to Unite educational programmes with its members, workplace representatives and other activists and, more generally, in colleges and universities; nothing like this work has been published before.

If we are to avoid the mistakes of the past it is of course essential that we understand the past – and learn from it!

This series of six books, detailing the history of one of the twentieth century's most important and vital trade unions, gives us that opportunity and I commend them to you.

Sharon Graham
General Secretary
Unite the Union

1

Setting the Scene

This final volume heralds the climax of deindustrialisation in every region and the rise of speculative finance capital. Employers created space for new types and ways of working that prized decentralised, even atomised workforces, nonetheless operating within tight constraints of poorly remunerated and exploited labour. To match this development, important segments of the labour movement were detached from traditional values to propose 'New' Labour, an apparently ideology-free concept based on Clintonesque 'triangulation' politics. The outcome was two decades when Labour politicians, apart from a handful of socialist MPs, distanced themselves from workers in struggle and many union leaders, desperate for a change in government, trailed after them.

The move from the 1980s into the 1990s marked a very difficult period for the unions – major defeats in the 1980s with the miners, twice with the print workers, the latter now part of Unite, at Eddie Shah's *Stockport Messenger* and at News International's Wapping plant, and the dockers' inability to resist the abolition of the National Dock Labour Scheme – created a situation where confidence was draining out of the movement. Notwithstanding Ron Todd's great personal standing within the T&G and the wider movement, Len McCluskey, who went on to become the first General Secretary of Unite, said in interview that it was his belief that after the miners' defeat, and with the demise of National Union of Mineworkers (NUM) General Secretary Arthur Scargill, there was no left leader across the whole of the trade union movement.

Even though the T&G was perceived as being a left of centre union, inside the union the left faction was not a national organisation, being mainly concentrated in Region 1 (London & the Home Counties), Region 6 (North West) and Region 7 (Scotland). In fact, the left only coalesced nationally, according to McCluskey, in the mid-1980s to work for Ron Todd's election as General Secretary in 1985.

In facing charges that his own election was flawed, by standing down and running successfully again, Todd had earned enormous respect for his integrity. He stayed loyal to the left, with its help weathering a brief period where right wingers sought to shackle the power of the General Secretary. Asked how he would like his stewardship of the union to be remembered, Ron Todd said: 'I would want the rank-and-file to say "He stayed true to the basic values of trade unionism"'.[1]

Facing retirement as the 1990s dawned, Ron Todd became concerned that the union had not changed enough to reflect the new workforce. It is clear that the nature of work and the workplace was changing fundamentally. Himself a product of progressive politics in Region 1, Todd was at the forefront of the push to recognise that Black workers were largely sidelined into inferior jobs in the workplace, even in well-organised plants like Ford Dagenham.

The Transition from Ron Todd to Bill Morris

During his term of office, Todd was acutely aware that the only Black officer, then a national secretary, was Bill Morris. Morris presented an image of being a hard worker; though Todd and others of his ilk had broken from it, the culture of important trade union officials was still largely steeped in convivial relations with employers with administrative skills low down in priority. There was scant use of any technology; everything went by post and progress was measured in months rather than weeks. Promising a refreshed union more open to a skills-based approach, Bill Morris was first appointed Deputy General Secretary and then received Todd's support to succeed him as General Secretary.

Andrew Murray in interview argued that, although Bill Morris was the candidate supported *by* the left he was not *of* the left. This highlighted a weakness in the left organisation across the union, brought about by the negative impact of industrial restructuring, that it could not generate its own candidate for General Secretary.

On becoming General Secretary, Bill Morris said that he wanted to be remembered as 'the man who rebuilt the modern T&G'.[2] His first big idea was to achieve a rapid and massive expansion of the union through merger. This was never to happen, and although subsequently a few tiny organisations did fall to the union, nothing of significance came across. We will return again to the T&G's merger strategy in Chapter 6.

1 *Daily Telegraph*, 6 March 1992.
2 *Voice*, 10 March 1992.

Crisis and Change in the T&G – the Klein Report

Trade union histories invariably focus on the paid, full-time leadership, as the previous passage has described with the transition from Ron Todd to Bill Morris. But at this point it is particularly necessary to highlight the work of one of the lay leaders of the union, Peter Hagger. Hagger was instrumental in every big decision in the union nationally, in Region 1 (still quaintly called London & the Home Counties) and in the taxi trade.

As Ken Livingstone recalls:

> The key to Ron's [Todd] election as General Secretary had been the work of Peter Hagger, a London taxi driver who was the organiser of the broad left inside the T&G executive and worked closely with me to ensure the success of the left inside the London Labour Party. When Peter suddenly died the left lost its sense of direction inside the T&G, but up until his death Pete was confident he would be able to deliver the T&G vote behind any left candidate for the Labour leadership.[3]

In the early 1990s, with the union in financial crisis, Andrew Murray notes:

> The Executive, pushed by Todd and his deputy Bill Morris, finally bit the bullet and agreed to cut the union's cloth according to circumstances, a painful process involving redundancies and office closures around the country. Leading Executive members from both right and left, most notably the highly influential London taxi driver Peter Hagger, having peered over the brink long enough, started to establish some form of consensus about taking the union forward.[4]

The way forward was that Bill Morris commissioned management consultants – Klein & Co – to conduct a root and branch review of the operation and structure of the union. The report drawn up by Klein & Co found that the union was 'too fragmented, with regions working as "mini-unions"', it was 'personnel heavy', decision-making was 'not properly co-ordinated' and was lacking in professionalism. Representation of women and ethnic minorities on committees was woefully under proportion to the membership numbers. The GEC was not 'sufficiently informed' when making decisions and the union was 'over-dependent' on membership contributions for its

---

3 K. Livingstone, *You Can't Say That: Memoirs* (Faber & Faber, 2011), pp.307–308.
4 A. Murray, *The T&G Story* (Lawrence & Wishart, 2008), p.179.

revenue. In rectifying these weaknesses, the consultant recommended that the aim should be to create a 'one union' culture.

Peter Hagger led a bipartisan team of lay members, known as the Executive Working Group, to shadow the consultants, touring Britain and Ireland, ensuring that the membership in the regions were fully briefed on the proposals for change.

Recognising that being organised in 11 regions, with the English regional boundaries seemingly drawn at random – they certainly followed no identifiable geographic or political logic – was dysfunctional, Peter ensured the adoption of the General Executive Council (GEC) recommendation, based on Klein's findings, at the Special Rules Conference held in December 1992 that the union should move from 11 to eight regions. Even though there was to be a *professionalisation* of Transport House, this single move, the merger of the regions, had the biggest impact on senior lay activists, those who sat on regional committees.

Regions 2 and 3, the South and South West, were merged, as were Regions 8, 9 and 10 – the North East (which included Cumbria), Yorkshire and the Humber. Of course there were now five of everything that had to be reduced to two, most particularly the regional secretaries. All were more or less to the right of the political divide in the T&G; in the new South & South West Region the genial Irishman John Ashman won out over the hard right John Joynson; in the new Northern Region Mike Davey, noted for his Catholicism, won out over right wingers Mal Snow and Joe Mills; Mills' main claim to fame was being 'Mr Fix It' during the parliamentary selection in Sedgefield Constituency Labour Party (CLP), a successful step on the ladder for Tony Blair, future prime minister.

There was also a growing culture of reliance on technical 'experts', as with the hiring of Peter Reignier, formerly an Austin Rover Finance Director, famed for a profit and loss mentality, and now in charge of financial decisions.

As the 1990s progressed, a clear line emerged in the union, with most national trade groups of the union increasingly proposing and leading a fighting-back union. Membership loss, coupled with administrative duplication and inefficiency, could no longer be financially sustained, leading to the significant internal changes described above. In the wake of this, many regions joined the General Secretary in favouring a cautious avoidance programme of not testing the anti-union laws and awaiting the return of a friendly government.

In interview Len McCluskey said that Bill Morris, after his election as General Secretary, was not particularly tolerant of dissent. He almost immediately sided with the right wing caucus of regional secretaries, and he took action against the left wing Region 6 in the North West. All of this precipitated a split in the left grouping within the union, typified as being between Region 6, the home region of McCluskey, and Region 1 led by

Barry Camfield and John Aitkin, Regional Secretary and GEC member respectively.

New Labour's mistakes, from miserly state pensions rises to the enthusiastic endorsement of the private finance initiative (PFI) in the National Health Service (NHS) – a hard-fought issue in the union – as if it were the embodiment of the socialist dream, and tolerance of 'liberal' imperialism led to a distinct but contested drift to the right in the union.

Voices from the Periphery

Almost unnoticed in all this was the case of Middlebrook Mushrooms in Yorkshire, which dismissed its employees, who were members of the T&G, in 1992.[5]

With roots in the mining community of Yorkshire, the 89 female mushroom pickers were sacked after refusing to take a cut in wages and accept inferior conditions, and the subsequent introducing of an overtime ban. Having accepted a pay freeze the previous year, the pickers were offered a 4 per cent increase in basic pay, but a massive reduction in overtime pay, leading to a 40 per cent cut in earnings. The company blamed the advent of Sunday trading, which meant more mushrooms had to be picked at weekends to satisfy the demands of supermarkets

But it devalued such excuses by its bizarre attitude to public relations. It had long sought to stand out by adopting a sponsorship approach to gaining publicity. At that time, Middlebrook was owned by the Booker group, which sponsored a prize for literature and had long supported a handicap prize at Catterick races, which provided much of its fertilising needs. The union reminded the media that this respected patron of the arts was previously a sugar plantation owner, an enthusiastic participant in the forcible transportation as slaves of Black people from Africa to the Caribbean two centuries before.

When the company heard that the workers were to hold a strike ballot, managers called the 89 pickers into the canteen on 20 November 1993 and told them they were being sacked and that they should leave the premises immediately. The factory lay in a hollow near the village of Whitley Bridge, with few employees walking to work; most were conveyed by minibus, with many of the women coming from mining families. For 15 months, enthusiastic picketing took place.

A plan to deposit a sizeable portion of manure on the doorstep of the Booker head office in London was modified. The union decided instead to protest by distributing leaflets outside supermarkets urging people not

---

5 See The Seventh Picket, *Our Bitter Harvest* (Sacked Mushroom Pickers' Support Fund, 1993).

to buy mushrooms. This in itself was not urging the public to breach a contract, but merely not to enter into a contract. They were not doing anything unlawful. Therefore, the Court of Appeal reversed an initial lower court decision, finding there was no unlawful means.[6]

Although too marginal from the union's overall activities, the experience was significant in terms of what was to come. A new generation of national officials had emerged who were radical and reforming, enablers of militancy at the least. The women of Middlebrook Mushrooms negotiated a solution satisfactory to them in the end but, although it was not immediately apparent, something fundamental had shifted.

When, 20 years earlier, feminists had sought to aid the organisation of women cleaners in central London, it could be written in retrospect that 'the byzantine rules of the T&G were double Dutch to us'.[7] Somehow, after the mushroom workers' dispute, it became a consensus that more needed to be done. Even at this stage, there was insistence on an evolutionary approach, avoiding mandatory seats for women, for example. By the end of the decade, the argument had been won.

Many Elections in Quick Succession and the Rise of Tony Woodley

Recognition of a constitutional role for the union's women members was not to the foreground as powerful men now jostled for position when Bill Morris was challenged in 1995 for his own job under Tory legislation that obliged periodic election.

At this point Peter Hagger, who was now Vice-Chair of the T&G GEC and a member of the Trades Union Congress (TUC) General Council, was becoming increasingly disillusioned with Bill Morris' support for Blair (or at least Gordon Brown) and Bill Clinton. Peter was actively considering standing against Morris, but illness struck him down. Laid low with cancer in 1994 he died on 26 February 1995.

Hagger had withdrawn his support for Morris; his subsequent pre-illness thoughts about taking on the role of challenger himself goes some distance to debunk Morris' biographer Geoffrey Goodman's claim that Hagger was about to 'sup with the devil' and form an anti-Morris alliance with arch right winger and Morris' former opponent for the position, Wales Regional Secretary George Wright: 'The anti-Morris group went as far as trying to persuade George Wright to stand again to remove Bill Morris ... But it backfired ... When approached by the Broad Left leader, Peter Hagger, George Wright flatly refused ...'.[8]

6 *Independent*, 24 July 1993.

7 S. Rowbotham 'Cleaners organising in Britain from the 1970s: a personal account', *Antipode*, 2006, vol.28, no.3.

8 G. Goodman, *Bill Morris: a Trade Union Miracle* (Arcadia Books, 2010), p.138.

Obituary — Peter Hagger (1944–1995)

Barry Camfield

The world outside the trade union movement knew little of Peter Hagger during his lifetime. And yet he has been correctly described as the most influential lay trade union activist in Britain.

This apparent contradiction can be explained by the fact that, despite the scale of his contribution to the Transport and General Workers' Union, Hagger was no glory-seeker. To him the movement itself — the ordinary members it represents — was more important than its leaders.

Beginning his working life as a computer engineer, Hagger became a London taxi-driver in 1969 and started activity in the Cab Section of the Transport and General Workers' Union in 1972. His leadership qualities soon became apparent and by the end of the decade he was Chair of our Region 1 Cab Trade Committee and a member of the T&G's General Executive Council. The 1980s saw him elected on to the General Council of the TUC, where he chaired the Joint Consultative Committee for the Trade Union Councils (local TUCs). More recently, he became Vice-Chair of our General Executive Council and, had he lived, he would almost certainly have succeeded the retiring incumbent, Dan Duffy, as Chair.

But a mere litany of the posts that Peter Hagger held can express neither the extent of his contribution nor his unique qualities. He was involved at all levels of the movement, at the same time combining work at leadership level with activity (sometimes of the most detailed kind) at the grassroots. It was he, for example, who first conceived of the Cost Index now used by the Department of Transport to determine the level of London taxi-fares each year. Either unpaid or at best receiving only expenses, he was utterly selfless in his contribution.

Through it all, Hagger never changed. Whether in discussion with general secretaries at the TUC General Council or talking to a potential recruit on a cab rank, he was the plain-speaking, working-class activist, and treated everyone the same, regardless of their position.

This is not to say that he lacked finesse. A Marxist, he shunned sectarianism and always aimed to build the maximum unity. Although he inevitably became embroiled in the T&G's internal disputes in the 1980s (during the course of which he was libelled by the Murdoch press) it was he who led the healing process. His gifted approach to tactics and his common sense were valued by many outside our own movement, as evidenced by the tributes paid to him by, for example, fleet taxi proprietors and vehicle manufacturers.

To those within the trade union movement, Peter Hagger's life and work serve as an inspiration and an example. And it is to be hoped that that his life and work will serve to expose, to others, the falsity of the usual caricatures of trade unionists.

7 March 1995[1]

1https://www.independent.co.uk/news/people/obituary-peter-hagger-1610215.html. See also B. Camfield, 'A dedication to Peter Hagger' in M. Davis & M. Mayo (eds), *Marxism & Struggle: Towards the Millennium* (Praxis Press, 1998), pp.1–4.

An early General Secretary re-election campaign in 1995 eventually saw Jack Dromey as the challenger to Morris. Dromey was widely perceived as being a Blairite candidate, despite protestations to the contrary. Goodman goes on to note:

> There was [an] important factor helping to persuade Dromey to pick up the challenge to Morris; he knew he could count on the backing of the Blair establishment in which his wife, Harriet Harman MP, was a prominent figure in the shadow cabinet team ... Blair enlisted one of his closest political and personal advisors, Peter Mandelson, to use his long-established media connections ... to filter the ... message in support of Jack Dromey.[9]

Having shored up a left profile in his core base and having won a second term, Morris, in response to the exceedingly limited gains unions were warned to expect from New Labour in government, increasingly backed a social partnership route, stating that he believed that 'partnership will increasingly focus in an international direction', mirroring the growth of global business.

From this point forward until the merger with Amicus to form Unite, executive officer elections in the T&G would no longer be fought between those described as being on the left and those labelled as being on the right of the union. The schism in the left was reflected in four successive elections.

First, on Communist Party member Jack Adams' retirement as Deputy General Secretary, the election in 1998 to replace him was contested by Fred Higgs and Margaret Prosser, both of whom claimed leftist credentials; Prosser was elected. Second, when Prosser retired in 2002 the contenders to replace her were former Vauxhall car worker from Ellesmere Port in the North West, National Secretary Tony Woodley, fresh from

9 Goodman, *Bill Morris*, p.138.

Rover Group, Longbridge

In the late 1990s, the purchase of Rover Group saw the Longbridge plant in Birmingham taken over by BMW. As European integration loomed, concerns came to the fore that deals between the UK, France, and Germany about the future path of the European Union (EU) would assign manufacturing to Germany, services and transport to France, with Britain focusing on finance and banking. Then in 2000 BMW wanted to sell Rover Cars to private equity group Alchemy Partners. Private equity was usually a cipher for asset stripping.

In their public statements Alchemy were open about their plans for large numbers of redundancies and retrenchment from the mass market to focus on low-volume MG sports cars. But Alchemy had no experience, no track record in either the specialist or mass car market.

In a separate part of the BMW withdrawal from the UK, Land Rover and Range Rover had already been earmarked for sale to the US car manufacturer Ford, who would include these brands in its premium car portfolio with Jaguar and Volvo.

A real fear of a closure of Longbridge plant had seen tension in the union leadership about the best way forward. But, as far as members were concerned, massive expressions of support were seen throughout the country, especially in the West Midlands, where 50,000 jobs in the supply chain were threatened.

Fearful of their small size in a progressively globalised car market, the German car maker had bought Rover Group and the Longbridge plant a few years before. However, continuing heavy losses alarmed BMW shareholders and the assets were put up for sale.

Another factor in the meltdown was the fact that it had not launched an all-new model since the Rover 75 more than six years earlier. In contrast, the likes of Ford and Vauxhall, and indeed most other Western European mass market carmakers, had replaced most if not all of their model ranges since the late 1990s.

The question of to whom to sell was the subject of a hotly contested difference between the union's General Secretary and the National Secretary of the Vehicle Building & Automotive Trade Group, Tony Woodley. Himself a former car worker, Woodley was adamant that the Phoenix Consortium be backed.

On 1 April the unions mobilised a huge demonstration of between 50,000 and 100,000 in support of continuing mass car manufacture at Longbridge and stopping the selloff of Longbridge to Alchemy.

A contemporary account of the demonstration, perhaps highlighting the differences between Morris and Woodley, records:

> Around the corner they were playing 'You'll Never Walk Alone', an emblem of Liverpool. T&GWU General Secretary Bill Morris took up the theme in his speech. The trouble was, his notorious oration to

the dockers four years ago ended on the identical phrase. Morris' performance on Saturday was, by comparison, very low key. It was the National Automotive Secretary, Tony Woodley who held the ring for the TGWU, despite a sometimes hostile reception.

The TGWU is still trying to find a new deal before time runs out around May 4, an interesting date for London voters as well. 'We're talking to BMW through the world's press here: you've got to negotiate a deal that we and British workers are prepared to accept. Not the sell-off that's presently on the table. Until we get that, there will be no peace for you and you company in this country'.[1]

Local journalist, Jon Griffin, reflecting on the demonstration writes: 'Twenty years later, I still think that the April 1 march was the turning point in the Save Rover campaign. It was the clearest manifestation of opposition to the private equity bid, the most concentrated public demonstration of support to save Longbridge as a mass employer'.[2]

The campaign to avoid break up saw the Longbridge manufacturing facility sold to the Phoenix Consortium, made up of former Rover managers, for the token sum of £10.

Like much of British industry, little modern investment in the plant had taken place and the company was running to stand still, running out of liquid capital within a few years. In April 2005, MG Rover group went into administration, leaving more than 6,000 workers without jobs.

Figure 1: Demonstration to save Longbridge car plant, 1 April 2000; in foreground Tony Woodley, short distance behind is Derek Robinson, former union convenor at Longbridge

1 G. Dropkin, *Rover Demo: a Glimmer of Hope (2000)* http://www.labournet.net/ukunion/0004/rover10.html.
2 J. Griffin (2020) https://www.inpublishing.co.uk/articles/business-matters-15262.

gaining a national profile with his campaign to save volume car production at Longbridge and the candidate of the Region 1 left faction, also a National Secretary, Peter Booth. The election was comfortably won by Woodley and, importantly, gave him further momentum for the future.

The big one was, of course, when Morris retired in 2003. Woodley had the momentum of recently winning the Deputy General Secretary election, but Len McCluskey recalls in interview that to be successful Woodley's team felt they would need an alliance with a wider group than just the supportive national officers; they met with Andrew Murray and Graham Stevenson to secure support from the Communist Party. In a showdown between the two left factions Woodley beat Barry Camfield for the General Secretaryship.

Woodley had also gained extra momentum with the rise of the 'awkward squad' – some of the small to mid-sized unions were electing leaders positioned more to the left than the prevailing trend in the unions and particularly in the Labour Party: Paul Mackney in the college teachers' union, the National Association of Teachers in Further & Higher Education (NATFHE) (now merged with the university teachers' union as the University and College Union (UCU)), Mark Serwotka in the civil servants' union, the Public & Commercial Services Union (PCS), Bob Crow in the National Union of Rail, Maritime & Transport Workers (RMT), and others.[10] This shift to the left and further disillusion with Labour increased after 2003 and the war in Iraq.

With the, at least in the immediate term, successful campaign at Longbridge and the shift in the political climate in the unions Woodley, as Andrew Murray says in interview, 'caught the breeze' that ensured his victory as General Secretary. Murray says of Camfield that, although clearly a progressive, he had become 'part of the scenery around Bill Morris, the continuity candidate'.

By way of an afterthought, there was a further Deputy General Secretary election to fill the vacancy created by Tony Woodley's election as General Secretary. Again the two factions were represented; the North West group by Graham Stevenson, the London group by Barry Camfield. In the event both were beaten by Jack Dromey who stayed in office until elected to the House of Commons as Labour MP for Birmingham Erdington in 2010, almost coinciding with the time that the T&G ceased to exist and Unite came into being as a major force in the national and international labour movement.

10 See A. Murray, *A New Labour Nightmare: the Return of the Awkward Squad* (Verso, 2003). See also the listing of 'awkward squad' members in J. McIlroy & G. Daniels, 'Organisation, Structure and Factionalism' in G. Daniels & J. McIlroy (eds), *Trade Unions in a New Neo-liberal World* (Routledge, 2008), p.150.

2

Militancy Resurgent but Problems with the Law

This chapter focuses on the two big industrial issues facing the union in the 1990s and into the twenty-first century. First, how were unions, including the T&G, to maintain militancy and support industrial action in the workplace in the face of ever more restrictive anti-union laws. We look at three major disputes that achieved national prominence in this period. Second, unions were under an ideological attack from a sophisticated new set of management techniques, known collectively by their Japanese name of *kanban*, that could wrongfoot unions and perhaps lead to their elimination from the workplace as unnecessary third parties in relations between management and workers.

Trade union freedoms were being curtailed through successive anti-union laws passed by the Conservatives since 1980, undermining trade unions' abilities to resist. The Conservatives had clearly learnt the lessons from Pentonville in the early 1970s when, by jailing five shop stewards, the law had in effect created martyrs; the blatant injustice of locking up trade union workplace leaders made it comparatively easy for the unions and the wider movement to mobilise support, up to the TUC threatening to call a general strike to secure the release of those imprisoned.

The new round of Conservative anti-union laws from the 1980s and into the 1990s proceeded on a step-by-step basis, rather like a salami slicer, gradually cutting back union rights. Further, the target of all of these laws, which sought to limit unions' immunity from civil action by employers, was union funds rather than officials, either lay or full time. Any breach of the law opened up a union's funds to damages claims by affected employers. Unlike Pentonville, a union could not in court now rely on on the fact that any action being complained about was being led by shop stewards and, therefore, outside the control of the union. Unions were made responsible for the actions of their lay officials, who may well not have followed the requirements of the new laws, unless the union *repudiated* any such action.

This was neo-liberalism on the offensive, ascendant and devastatingly destructive for the trade union movement. 'This tore the guts out of existing union organisation and sapped the willingness to fight of those lucky enough to remain in employment'[1] as Andrew Murray so clearly summarised the situation at this period.

Tensions between the left in the union and Bill Morris as General Secretary became more apparent. It became a challenge to maintain militancy in the union, which would have often meant challenging the anti-union laws when members were threatened by them. A risk-averse outlook prevailed aimed at protecting what increasingly became defined as the *fabric of the union*.

Against the modern way of partnership was the observable, increasing irritation of members, anxious for lay member control and the tradition of fighting back. However, fighting back in the last two decades of the T&G was fraught with legal difficulties. The legal situation could sway the manner in which the union responded to members in struggle, often depending on the point of view of the union's leadership.

Mersey Docks & Harbour Co, British Airways and Friction Dynamics

Three major industrial disputes either side of the millennium brought these difficulties into sharp relief. These were on the Liverpool docks 1995–1998, British Airways (BA) cabin crew in 1997 and, Friction Dynamics in north Wales in 2001. Liverpool docks and Heathrow airport, where our first two examples are located, are those workplaces described by John Foster in an earlier volume of this series as 'fortresses of the working class'.

From the start it was clear that the Liverpool dockers were taking action that was outside the very restrictive anti-trade union laws in operation in Britain. By being outside the civil law, and thereby possibly leaving the union open to damages claims by the port employers, the union steadfastly declined to make the strike official. Eventually, after two years and more, the dockers were beaten.

There is a great irony connected with the Liverpool dock strike. In the formative years leading to the foundation of the T&G, a generation of dockers' union leaders from the Great Dock Strike gained national and international prominence, most particularly Tom Mann. One of Mann's great achievements, in the closing years on the nineteenth century, was to be a leader in the foundation of the International Transport Workers' Federation (ITF). During the 1930s the ITF was very active in

---

1 Murray, *The T&G Story*, p.171.

anti-colonial and anti-racist work, even infiltrating Nazi Germany from 1933 to maintain an underground trade union network. But by the turn of the twentieth century it had become more cautious in its approach. The Liverpool docks strike created an existential crisis for the ITF as T&G dockers, members of the union that was the midwife to its foundation, sought to break away from what they believed to be a federation incapable of generating international solidarity, and formed their own dockers' international, the International Dockworkers' Council.

Legally, more or less the opposite was the case with the BA cabin crew. The union's members were very clearly inside the strictures of the trade union laws, even though BA threatened individual members with legal proceedings for breach of contract if they joined the strike. The dispute was fully backed by the union with the then General Secretary, Bill Morris, involved towards the end, in a dispute that was seemingly a victory for the T&G.

The Friction Dynamics dispute was compliant with the anti-union laws, so there was no chance, in the first instance, of the union being sued. The dispute was fully backed by the union, with the support of the then General Secretary, Bill Morris, and subsequently the incoming General Secretary, Tony Woodley. Even though they started from a position within the law, the workers were ultimately undone by the law, favouring as it does the employer over workers and unions in almost all cases.

Liverpool Docks[2]

From 1995 there was a massive blow to social partnership, exemplified by the struggle of the Liverpool dockers. They and their supporters in the union showed how traditional solidarity in a globalised economy should be maintained, during a dispute of 28 months up to 1998 that triggered support around the world.

Dock work had traditionally been an industry based on casual labour, marked by work often only being available to those who had curried favour with the foreman with a pint of beer in the pub. Even the Great Dock Strike of 1889 was a strike about the rate for the job – the Dockers' Tanner – not about permanent employment.

The period after the Second World War was marked by strikes on the docks. One consequence of the strikes was the establishment of the National Dock Labour Scheme, which aimed to eliminate casual working from the industry. That did not happen, so in the mid-1960s

---

2 For a comprehensive, partisan history of the Liverpool docks dispute, 1995–1998, see M. Carden, *Liverpool Dockers: a History of Rebellion and Betrayal* (Carden Press, 2022).

Figure 2:
Demonstration
in support of the
sacked Liverpool
dockers, 23 March
1996

the government appointed a committee of inquiry under Lord Devlin to examine, among other matters, casual working in the docks.

However, Devlin's attempt at the elimination of casual working was incompatible with the pace of technological change, particularly containerisation, which led inevitably to the effective return of casual working in most of the ports. 'The docks industry was finally decasualised in 1967. However, by 1970 with dock and lighterage companies going out of business, hundreds of dock workers were returned to the NDLB [National Dock Labour Board] Temporary Unattached Register, casual working again'.[3]

3 K. Hussey & A. Weir, 'From Pentonville to P&O: the wrong arm of the law', *Labour Outlook*, 2022, https://labouroutlook.org/2022/07/24/from-pentonville-to-po-the-wrong-arm-of-the-law.

Throughout the 1970s and 1980s there was an exodus of dock workers from the industry. For those who remained the scheme was valued and seen as some sort of job guarantee. Certainly it was protection enough for the port employers to secure from the Conservative government parliamentary time in 1989 to ensure the passage of legislation to abolish the scheme. For all of Secretary of State Norman Fowler's protestations to the contrary, the abolition of the scheme marked the return of casual working to the ports. Also, workers exiting the industry and scheme abolition facilitated a tremendous increase in port employers' profits, most certainly including in Liverpool.

> Between 1989 and 1995, the number of employees at Mersey Docks & Harbour Company dropped from 1100 to 500 … Rationalisation proved to be lucrative for MDHC [Mersey Docks & Harbour Company], as annual profits rose nearly 10-fold from £3.1 million in 1986 to £29.6 million in 1996. The number of dockers may have been vanishing from the waterfront, but MDHC's profits soared during this period.[4]

The issue that sparked the dispute in Liverpool flowed directly from the return to casual working. The dockers who remained employed by MDHC were mostly older men who would have been previously employed when the scheme was still operational. Torside, the firm originally at the centre of the dispute, was not a stevedoring firm but a labour supply agency, a business practice unknown under the scheme. It was supplying younger, inexperienced and lower paid dock workers to replace the older ex-scheme dockers as they retired from the industry:

The dispute began when Torside dismissed five workers who had questioned overtime payments with the company. The five dismissed threw up a picket line, which was honoured by their colleagues working for Torside. The company then, on 25 September 1995, dismissed 80 Torside workers who refused to cross the picket line. Two days later those dismissed mounted a picket at Seaforth container terminal; their slogan being 'Save the 80 – Say No To Casuals'. On 29 September 400 dockers employed by MDHC were dismissed for refusing to cross the Torside picket.

So began the lengthy dispute between the dockers and MDHC. Though often seen as a strike, it was really a lockout and mass dismissal. MDHC actually sacked the dockers for breach of contract when they refused to cross the picket line of Torside workers. A mature, experienced and skilled workforce (the dockers had previously been described by *Lloyd's List* as 'the most productive workforce in Europe'), their solidarity with Torside

---

4 B. Marren, 'The Liverpool Dock Strike, 1995–98: a resurgence of solidarity in the age of globalisation', *Labor History*, 2016, pp.463–481.

workers was focused on sympathy for the outsourced, younger workers forced to accept poorer wages and terms and conditions.

The union's position throughout was that, as the dockers had taken their action outside the law – no secret postal ballot, no notice given to the employer and so on – it was legally impossible to endorse the dispute. Endorsement would have not only allowed for regular financial support for the dockers (although the GEC did authorise hardship payments), but international support from overseas dock workers' and seafarers' unions could have been requested on an official basis. Endorsement was refused to protect the 'fabric of the union', to guard against possible sequestration of the union's assets.

By December the dispute had acquired a global dimension when three Liverpool dockers picketed the container terminal in New York, which the American dockers would not cross, prompting the Atlantic Container Line to threaten to pull out of Liverpool.

The dispute ground on from 1995 into 1996 and 1997. There were weekly meetings at which the dockers voted whether to continue or not; inevitably the answer was 'yes'.

The dispute threw up many interesting new developments, including the way in which international solidarity could be mobilised. Although they did not know it at the time, this was an early dispute in the internet age; e-mail and fax machines meant that the dockers in Liverpool could immediately contact dockers' unions wherever in the world without such contact being mediated by either the T&G or the dockers' global union federation, the ITF. The internet age provided an easy opportunity for horizontal contacts between groups of workers rather than relying on vertical structures through the unions.

On 17 February 1996, and for five days subsequently, under the auspices of the Liverpool dockers and responding to invitations issued by fax or via the internet, the First International Conference of Port Workers was held in Liverpool Town Hall, attracting 53 delegates from 15 countries and from as far afield as Australia and the US. Carden notes: 'The conference decided, among other matters, to establish an alternative international dockworkers' organisation'.[5]

However, at that stage this may have been more aspirational than realistic. A second conference was convened on 31 August and 1 September, held in the Unemployed Workers' Centre in Liverpool. An international day of action was called for, to coincide with the first anniversary of the dispute. Among other actions there was a 24-hour stoppage by tug boat crews on the Mersey; there was a 24-hour boycott of all Atlantic Container Line ships in Sweden; and a march and rally in Liverpool attended by 10,000 supporters.

5 Carden, *Liverpool Dockers*, p.248.

Two months later on 26 October dockers from 18 ports across ten countries attended a meeting in Paris to further support the Liverpool dockers. Now known as the Dockers' Steering Committee this was clearly a step to forming the alternative international to the ITF. In fact the meeting changed its name to the International Dockworkers' Council (IDC) and got off to a flying start:

> Within a day of the IDC forming, 4,000 dockers throughout Spain ... had paralysed ports for one hour in solidarity with Liverpool, and as a warning shot to their own employers and government ... The Spanish unions demanded the reinstatement of the sacked Liverpool men, and sought a negotiating framework to guarantee that workers in Spain would not experience the same fate as their Liverpool comrades.[6]

By the time of the second conference of the IDC, in Montreal on 25 May 1997, it was clear that the organisation was indeed an alternative international, with delegates attending from around the world; including the Netherlands, Portugal, Spain, New Zealand, South Africa, Japan and Russia. The purpose of the conference was twofold: first to target the largest shipping lines in the port of Liverpool, Atlantic Container Lines and Cast and, second, to mobilise against the global casualisation of dock work.

During the miners' strike of 1984–1985 there had been established a women's support group, Women Against Pit Closures. Here on the docks, an overwhelming male occupation, a similar group was established, Women of the Waterfront, which, like the miners' support group, was active in organising fundraising, organising and attending demonstrations, meetings and pickets and generally being a positive not passive support group for the dockers. Led by Doreen McNally, many of these women would have had memories of the irregular pay and poor working conditions on the docks in the era of casual working.

It may have been imagined that the Labour landslide in the May 1997 general election would have brought some relief for the dockers. But it soon became clear that the Labour government would not be persuaded to use its 'golden share', a holding in the equity of MDHC, to intervene on the part of the dockers, or, as it turned out, to support any other group of workers in struggle.

In the opinion of Liverpool docker participant/historian Mike Carden:

> As the trade union and labour movement sought to disconnect itself from their historic roots the dockers were portrayed as being

---

6 Carden, *Liverpool Dockers*, p.347.

locked in a form of trade unionism from another century – a class of workers that had long-faded into the mists of the past; like a lost memory of a history without relevance or meaning in modern times – a forgotten civilisation. From the 1980s onwards, the working class and their communities had become identified as a political liability.[7]

The dispute was called off on 26 January 1998 when the dockers accepted an offer from MDHC. Not a single docker got his job back, but the settlement did include continuity of pensions. The settlement only covered about two-thirds of the dockers; the remaining one-third were supported by money raised from benefit gigs and record sales.

Andrew Murray notes: 'the T&G leadership made every effort to support the locked out dockers within the tightly drawn framework of the law. They were given considerable material support, but no industrial solidarity or other action that, in Morris's view, could have exposed the union to the threat of considerable losses as a result of legal proceedings'.[8] The docks dispute in Liverpool had driven a wedge between many lay activists and others on the left and the leadership of the union.

At the 37th Biennial Delegates' Conference (BDC) (1997) an executive statement covering the dispute was put to the conference that Jack Adams, Deputy General Secretary (and a member of the Communist Party) had the unenviable task of moving. The statement listed in great detail all that the union has done to support the sacked dockers, other than make the dispute official. The key section of the statement argued: 'Council has a clear responsibility to preserve the fabric of the union and operate within the constraints of the law. To undertake the action recommended [in a number of motions] would not only breach current BDC policy, but would result in the union losing any immunity from legal challenge, leaving the fabric of the organisation vulnerable'.[9]

The executive statement was lost when put to a vote of the BDC. However, the delegates could not really decide on which position they wished to pursue – full tilt support for the dockers or back the cautious line being followed by the leadership. Eight motions were debated after the executive statement fell, but the six motions seeking to make the dispute official, or variations on that theme, were lost. The two that were carried called for actions that, if not unachievable, were certainly not deliverable in the short term – a return to registered dock work and for government intervention in the dispute.

7 Carden, *Liverpool Dockers*, p.xvii.
8 Murray, *The T&G Story*, p.193.
9 Minutes of the Proceedings of the 37th Biennial Delegate Conference 1997, p.19.

Bill Morris in the *T&G Record* on the Liverpool Docks Dispute

The following article, in the name of Bill Morris, appeared in the February–March 1997 issue of the *TGWU Record*, the official publication of the union.

Setting the record straight

The TGWU has been heavily criticised in some parts of the media over its role in the Liverpool docks dispute. Bill Morris sets the record straight.

The dispute on the Liverpool Docks has been running for nearly eighteen months. It has its origins in the dismissal of 80 dockworkers by Torside Ltd., a company which operates in the docks, following a dispute concerning overtime payments which led to the sacking of five men.

The Torside employees then decided to mount a picket of the dock, directed at employees of the Mersey Docks and Harbour Company, demanding that MDHC take responsibility for their re-engagement. In doing so, they disregarded the advice of the deputy general secretary of the union, Jack Adams, who warned that this could lead to further sackings.

This is what happened – the MDHC dismissed 320 (sic) of its own employees who refused to cross the picket line mounted by the Torside workers. Because the MDHC workers were not in direct dispute with their own employer, and had broken their contract of employment without first holding an industrial action ballot, the TGWU became vulnerable to legal action for damages by MDHC or any ship owner.

The union's biennial delegate conference has made it clear that while we operate under draconian Tory legislation designed to weaken legitimate trade union activity, the leadership of the union has an obligation to preserve the fabric of the TGWU and not engage in activities for which it has no immunity or legal protection.

This is not a position any trade union would wish to be in. Everyone would wish to be able to give full support to any group of members unjustly dismissed, as the Liverpool dockers have been. However the TGWU has an obligation to all its 900,000 members, which must include avoiding action which could render the union unable to operate on behalf of those members.

In that context, we have had to be particularly mindful of protecting the future of the 1,000 TGWU members still employed by MDHC and not involved in the present dispute.

Nevertheless the union has endeavoured to give our members in Liverpool whatever support it can. This has included:

- Establishing and maintaining negotiations with MDHC, which have led to the present offer of 41 jobs back, £28,000 redundancy payments for each of those who leave, and full pension rights. As part of the agreement, this offer is to be put to a secret ballot of those involved.

- Supporting the community hardship fund established in Liverpool with donations of over £500,000 from the union's central fund alone, and urged support for this fund from TGWU branches and other unions at home and abroad.

- Helped develop proposals for a workers' co-operative to guarantee employment for dockers on Merseyside.

- Worked with the International Transport Workers Federation to campaign for the dockers' reinstatement within the bounds of what is legal and practicable.

These facts give the lie to the theme being developed by a few ultra-left journalists that the TGWU has abandoned its responsibilities in relation to the Liverpool dockers. The Guardian, in particular, has given space to attacks on the union and its leadership, yet has failed to print in full letters of rebuttal submitted to it. These letters are reproduced here.

From Bill Morris:
'The unofficial action which resulted in the employer being able to use Tory legislation to sack the dockers thwarted the union's ability to intervene.'

John Pilger is entitled to his opinions, even though it is surprising that the Guardian should give so much space to the banal view that all the problems of the last 17 years can be laid at the door of 'the timidity of union barons'. He is not however entitled to maliciously represent the position of the TGWU in general, nor in relation to the Liverpool Docks dispute in particular.

Firstly, it is absurd to assert that the TGWU made 'no sustained attempt' to oppose the abolition of the National Dock Labour Scheme in 1989. For several months we did little else, both politically and industrially, despite the difficulties posed by the Tory anti-union legislation which Pilger so blithely ignores. Subsequently, we also funded the longest industrial tribunal unfair dismissal case in history which resulted in the Tilbury dockers proving their case, an outcome totally ignored by the employers.

Secondly, it is a slander on the union to allege that we have an 'unspoken sweetheart agreement' with employers in the Liverpool docks. Presumably, Pilger feels that the word 'unspoken' absolves him from the need to provide any evidence. The fact is that on the Liverpool docks, as elsewhere, the TGWU works solely for the interests of its members under the most difficult of circumstances.

Thirdly, let us have some simple truth here about numbers. Of the 1,000 TGWU members employed by the Merseyside [sic] Docks and Harbour Company, 328 were dismissed; 80 others were employed by a separate company, Torside.

Fourthly, Pilger seeks to make much of my reluctance to be interviewed by him, a reluctance more than justified by the anti-TGWU bile which suffuses from his article. He would have been more honest had he referred to his own aggressive refusal to submit written questions when this was offered by the union's press officer – possibly because unambiguous answers which could not be twisted may not have suited his pre-determined thesis.

Fifthly, Pilger alleges that I called the dockers' leaders to London to tell them to abandon their struggle. This is a direct lie. Far from any notion of abandoning the struggle, the purpose was to define our tactics for the round of negotiations which were pending and which were to be led by the deputy general secretary.

The unofficial action which resulted in the employer being able to use Tory legislation to sack the dockers thwarted the union's ability to intervene and, indeed, we have had to defend writs served on the union both at home and in the American courts. Despite all of this, the TGWU has worked closely with the shop stewards and insisted that they be involved in all the talks to find a negotiated settlement to the dispute. One of the difficulties in resolving this dispute, which John Pilger seems to ignore, is the demand by the shop stewards that 80 men, who never worked for the company in the first place, must be employed by Mersey Docks and Harbour Company as part of the settlement.

Additionally, our efforts to secure a dialogue and negotiated settlement with the employers are continuing, as is the support which the TGWU has given to the community fund established on Merseyside to relieve hardship amongst dockers' families.

Finally, which Pilger writes that 'for much of its history the TGWU... has served the aims of the British establishment' he slanders the lives and work of the millions of British men and women have built up this union as a democratic working class organisation fighting for social justice. Perhaps he should explain why the establishment has devoted so much time and energy to undermining unions like the TGWU over the last 17 years. Our survival owes nothing to the advice of John Pilger and the like.

If John Pilger's article serves any purpose it is only in reminding us that ultra-left politics so often end up in the same place as the policies of the right – attacking the organisations of the labour movement.

ITF to the Guardian:
In the Saturday weekend supplement there was an article by John Pilger about the Liverpool dockers' strike. The International Transport Workers' Federation (ITF) wishes to correct a factual error that was reproduced.

It is not true that the ITF stopped Belgian and German unions from going to Liverpool.

Without going into the complex history of the dispute, which is cur
rently at a sensitive stage, we would like to make clear the following:

- the ITF, like our affiliate the TGWU, has strongly supported the Liverpool dockers' demands for reinstatement from the beginning and, within the bounds of what is legally and practically possible, we continue to do so.

- the ITF has never, would never, and is constitutionally incapable of 'stopping affiliates from attending a conference'. The unions involved are perfectly capable of making up their own minds whether or not to accept an invitation and in the present case, neither the Belgian nor the German unions promised to attend;

- ITF unions have contributed substantially to the Liverpool dockers, including donations from the BTB, the ÖTV and directly from the ITF Solidarity Fund.

We all want this dispute ended soon on terms acceptable to the dockers. The TGWU, the TUC and the ITF are all doing everything they can to achieve this objective. The idea that total victory was somehow snatched from their grasp because a couple of people did not show up at a conference in August is, frankly, ridiculous.

We were not contacted by the journalist who wrote this article and we would have been very happy to talk about this dispute and the many similar situations that are happening globally. One of the major reasons that the Liverpool strikers have received so much support throughout the world is because dock workers' unions can see that what is happening in Liverpool is being tried by port employers all over the world.

From David Cockcroft (International Transport Workers Federation general secretary), Bob Baete (Belgian transport workers' national secretary), and Manfred Rosenberg (German dockers' secretary)

From Bill Morris to the Guardian:
The Merseyside Port Shop Stewards assert that there is no difference between the positions of the employer and the TGWU in the Liverpool docks dispute and that there is little hope of a negotiated settlement to the dispute.

These two false positions add up to a counsel of despair. Firstly, the shop stewards are well aware of the support given to them by their union, notwithstanding the fact that the dispute falls foul of the draconian anti-union legislation passed over the last 17 years, a fact many of the TGWU's critics simply ignore.

Secondly, there is no realistic way this dispute – like most disputes – will end without a negotiated settlement. That is why the TGWU has put so much effort into working for an acceptable agreement aimed at ending a dispute which has damaged the Liverpool docks and the whole Merseyside community, as well as the interests of our unjustly dismissed members.

> In taking the position we have, the TGWU leadership has discharged its obligation to the union as a whole, in protecting our assets from sequestration, and to all our members employed at the Liverpool docks, including the 900 who have continued working throughout this dispute.

British Airways Cabin Crew

BA cabin crew held a three-day global stoppage in a 1997 protest at massive funding cuts of more than $70 million from cabin crew operations as part of BA Chief Executive Robert Ayling's plan to save $1.7 billion by the year 2000. Dramatic displays of solidarity in airports across the world saw thousands of planes grounded, frustrating the company's attempts to ride out the strike.

Figure 3: BASSA pickets, Heathrow Airport, July 1997

Cabin crew in what was then the two national flag carriers had been union organised since the 1950s, before the British Overseas Airways Corporation (BOAC) and British European Airways (BEA) merger that created BA. By the late 1980s BA cabin crew were organised in two branches of T&G/BASSA (British Airlines Stewards & Stewardesses Association), one branch for long haul reflecting its BOAC origins and one branch for short haul reflecting its BEA origins. Eventually, the two BA cabin crew branches merged, with sub-sections for wide-bodied and short-haul crew, as the T&G 1/2000 BASSA branch.

In 1988 BA took over British Caledonian, essentially a long-haul airline, whose cabin crew were also organised by the T&G, but in a separate branch of the union. British Caledonian had established 'co-operative industrial relations' since the early 1980s, whereas at BA it was not always so harmonious between the employer and both baggage handlers and cabin crew. The merger of the British Caledonian and BA cabin crew union branches did not proceed smoothly, with the leadership of the former British Caledonian branch definitely an irritant to the process.

In 1989, with the active support of the pilots' union, BALPA (the British Airline Pilots' Association), BA management and some British Caledonian union activists, a split was engineered and the 'moderate' union Cabin Crew '89 was launched, primarily based among long-haul members. Remarkably, defending the union's position against the breakaway the T&G found itself in the High Court defending a libel allegation.

BA management clearly hoped that Cabin Crew '89 would be the Union of Democratic Mineworkers for the aviation industry, a house union that would undermine the solidarity and integrity of independent cabin crew union organisation. In 1999 Cabin Crew '89 became part of the Amalgamated Engineering & Electrical Union (AEEU), the predecessor union of Amicus, that was then in the process of hoovering up small, often right wing, professional unions and staff associations. Cabin Crew '89 was a Trojan Horse during the 1997 strike, signing a separate deal with BA. It remained problematic until the formation of Unite, when it was reintegrated into the BASSA organisation.

During the 1980s BA faced two challenges to its operating environment. First, the Thatcher government, with its neo-liberal zeal, was ideologically committed to privatising state assets, BA was no exception. Second, many legislatures, including the EU, were intent on deregulating the civil aviation market, to move to open skies, to allow challenger airlines entry to the market to compete with the likes of BA.

To be 'fit' for privatisation BA needed to be turned into a profitable operation; part of the management prescription to achieve this was a change in culture, to gain greater identification with corporate goals by its employees. 'At the heart of this was the *Putting People First* training programme launched by Colin Marshall, the company's new chief executive, in December 1983'.[10] Essentially, 'the foundation of BA's competitive strategy, which can be traced back to the 1980s, was to reorient the company's business, and the mindset of its managers, from transportation to service'.[11]

Throughout the 1980s and 1990s, other aspects of the company's operation were changed to fit with the service delivery model. Personnel was renamed 'Human Resources'; its work in promoting culture change involved the classic traits of total quality management (more of which later). The Marshall era at BA turned it from a loss maker to one of the most profitable in world; the *Putting People First* regime had allegedly turned the company culture from one vaguely militaristic to one allegedly people centred.

Maybe *Putting People First* had been deemed a success because it was accompanied by certain assurances about job security; if your job had not been outsourced that is. It could not last. Marshall left to be replaced by Bob Ayling as CEO in 1995. Deregulation and the rise of the no-frills, low-cost airlines challenged BA's profitability. If *Putting People First* had been a revolution in how employees were managed, Ayling demanded that there should be a second revolution within the airline.

Ayling was operating with the parameters identified by Bamber and his colleagues, who noted:

In the post-World War II period most of the main legacy airlines in countries other than the USA were at least partly owned by governments, were highly regulated and were seen as providing a form of *public* transport. However, since the 1980s, many of these airlines have been privatised and their markets at least partly de-regulated. Against this background, such legacies have been increasingly concerned with maximising shareholder value in the short term and have become tougher employers, with a tendency for cost competitiveness strategies to focus to a greater extent on reducing employees' economic rewards and other benefits.[12]

Ayling proposed to cut £1 billion of spending across the whole organisation; including 5,000 voluntary redundancies to be replaced by new entrants on lower pay and conditions. Outsourcing was to continue, with

10 C. Grugulis & A. Wilkinson, 'Managing culture at British Airways; hype, hope and reality', *Long Range Planning*, 2002, vol.35, no.2, pp.179–194.

11 P. Turnbull et al., 'Strategic choice and industrial relations; a case study of British Airways' (n.d.) https://citeseerx.ist.psu.edu/viewdoc/download?doi=10.1.1.461.1450&rep=rep.1&type=pdf.

12 G.J. Bamber et al., 'Contrasting management and employment relations strategies in European airlines', *Journal of Industrial Relations*, 2009, vol.51, no.5, pp 635–652. Emphasis in original.

the idea of perhaps becoming a virtual airline. Ayling sought to benchmark all corporate activities against a so-called 'market price', the price at which BA could obtain the same function on the open market. If the internal price could not be driven down to the 'market price' then the function would be franchised (other airlines with aircraft painted in BA livery) or sub-contracted (catering).

For cabin crew, Ayling proposed to buy out a number of allowances in return for a higher rate of basic pay, but only with a three-year guarantee that no member of crew would be worse off. The sweetheart union, Cabin Crew '89, voted to accept BA's offer; the T&G threatened strike action.

Industrial relations academic Peter Turnbull notes the views of crew leading up to the strike:

> [W]e've all been through PPF [*Putting People First*] and other programmes, been told we're the best thing since sliced bread, and now they're saying they're not sure whether they even want to employ you anymore. There's no longer any trust in management … Customer service and good employee relations go hand in hand. But all BA want is the customer service, they've dismissed the idea of good employee relations.[13]

The strike ballot returned a 73 per cent mandate for strike action on an 80 per cent turn out. A three-day strike was called for 9 July 1997. BA management contacted union members at home, threatening action in the courts for breach of contract if members went on strike. On the appointed day 300 members were reported as being on strike but 2,000 reported in sick. This level of absence obviously more or less grounded BA worldwide.

Bill Morris wrote to Ayling offering talks, a move he announced to the media. Ayling agreed even before receipt of Morris' letter. In the settlement the T&G agreed that there would be cost savings of £42 million including the contracting out of the catering operation. Although existing crew won the case that their terms and conditions would not be slashed, and union membership rocketed to bring T&G/BASSA membership to over 10,000, many established crew members resigned over the next year or two to be replaced by new entrants on lower terms and conditions.

The strike cost BA £125 million. Profits subsequently slumped – in the next two years they fell by 61 per cent and in 2000 BA announced losses of £224 million. On 10 March 2000, Ayling resigned as CEO.

In the context of the time, in the dying days of John Major's lame-duck Conservative government 'the company came to an agreement with the union … representing a rare high-profile victory for the T&G in the 1990s,

---

13 Turnbull, 'Strategic choice and industrial relations'.

and a personal success both for Bill Morris and for the national secretary for the industry, George Ryde, who had led from the front'.[14]

Given the massive stay away from work for whatever reason in July 1997, we must conclude that as far as employees were concerned *Putting People First* was really just another management strategy aimed at shaping the behaviour and allegiance of the workforce. 'BA's programme of culture change was not an expression of mutual trust and reciprocal emotional obligation between the company's employees and its management. Rather, it was an alternative control mechanism and should be understood as such'.[15]

Friction Dynamics

The factory in Caernarfon opened in 1964, producing brake linings for the auto industry. It was part of the Ferodo company, which became a subsidiary of Turner & Newell in 1926, and which in turn, in 1998, had become part of the US-based Federal Mogul corporation. Brake linings at the time were manufactured from asbestos and, with ever increasing damages claims from workers killed or maimed from asbestos-related illness, it became clear to workers in Caernarfon that Turner & Newell were running down the factory with the intention of getting out of the business.

Pritchard and Edwards observed: 'it became obvious that Turner Newell's intention was to pull out of Ferodo over a long and painful period with less and less investment in the factory. And to make matters worse, from the workers' view point in particular, the close relationship that had existed between the unions and management was destroyed'.[16]

In 1997, an American businessman, Craig Smith, strong armed the Welsh Development Agency into making grants available for him to purchase the factory in Caernarfon, to be renamed Friction Dynamics.

From today's perspective it is clear that Smith had as his intention to break union organisation in the factory, particularly the T&G, which was by far the largest union present. 'Smith intended to break the strength of the union by provoking the members to breaking point and trampling on their rights as workers. One example was the case in 1999 when Smith awarded a pay rise to all workers except the T&G members'.[17]

This was an early indication that employment rights mattered little to Smith, as this initial skirmish probably put him outside the terms of section 146 of the Trade Union and Labour Relations (Consolidation) Act

14 Murray, *The T&G Story*, p.194.
15 Grugulis & Wilkinson, 'Managing culture at British Airways'.
16 T. Pritchard & I. Edwards, *On the Line: the Story of the Friction Dynamics Workers* (T&G Cymru/Wales, 2005), p.17.
17 Pritchard & Edwards, *On the Line*, p.20.

1992, which outlaws acts of detriment that prevent or deter a worker from becoming a member of a union or *penalising him for doing so* (my emphasis).

Smith further put himself in breach of the same law when, in January 2001, via the company notice board, he announced a change to the holiday arrangements, which meant that T&G members would have to take their holiday entitlement on Mondays only – in other words a two-week holiday would have to be taken on ten consecutive Mondays.

Clearly this was a provocative act by Smith, who hoped the union would opt for the wildcat option – no ballot, just walking out – which would have possibly allowed him to sue for breach of the anti-union laws. The members were keen for a wildcat strike, but were dissuaded by the local full-time official, Tom Jones.

One of the union's members, Gwilym Williams, reflected on the new situation: 'we were probably swayed somewhat because we wanted the new order to be a new start for us. Everyone wanted to believe that this was a new beginning for the factory, and that possibly meant that we failed to see the warning signs to begin with'.[18]

By February the provocation was racked up a further notch when 25 workers were declared redundant, allegedly because of low sales figures. All of those to be dismissed were members of the T&G. Not only was this a full-frontal assault on the T&G's members, but it was also an attack on the T&G because the number of redundancies could have, in the shop stewards' opinion, reduced the union's density to a such a low level that Smith may have been able to derecognise the union.

Jones had to organise a ballot for industrial action. In it 92 per cent of T&G members voted 'yes'. In April 2001 the strike began, initially for one week. The strikers attempted to return to work on 10 May but the management refused them access to the plant, so in other words, technically, the dispute had become a lockout but was still seen essentially as a strike.

It had always been the case that if a worker went on strike it was invariably a breach of the contract of employment and an employer could lawfully dismiss the striking worker. We have noted previously that in 1997 BA managers contacted cabin crew at home, threatening that if crew members joined the strike BA would take action in the courts for breach of contract. This was probably unlikely, but was deployed as a form of intimidation.

The incoming Blair government of 1997 promised, and made, very modest changes to trade union and workers' rights. But in a seemingly positive move by the Labour government, with the Employment Relations Act 1999 strikers were to be given protection from dismissal for eight weeks from the commencement of a strike, subsequently increased to 12 weeks.

18 Pritchard & Edwards, *On the Line*, p.33.

As this dispute dragged on for almost three years, protection for eight weeks against dismissal by the employer was not particularly helpful. But, even though the eight weeks was generally not too highly prized, in an exchange between the owner Craig Smith and Dafydd Wigley AM, the local Plaid Cymru Welsh Assembly member, Smith made an injudicious comment, as Wigley pointed out:

> I received a reply from Smith in a letter, albeit signed by his secretary, which said something like, 'in any case I have already hired a new labour force'. This was about four weeks into the strike and so that sentence became absolutely critical in the [Tribunal] hearing, since it proved to all intents that he'd dismissed his workers well before the end of the eight weeks.[19]

In July 2001 the strikers all received their P45s through the post; in this matter at least Smith was a man of his word and indeed had dismissed all those on strike.

The preliminaries of the Employment Tribunal case were heard in the Caernarfon County Court in November 2001. Following an application from Smith to move proceedings away from the locality, a date was set for the full hearing, almost a year later in October 2002, in Liverpool. All the while picketing was maintained outside the factory; a Christmas 2001 delivery of meat and produce was made, donated by porters – T&G members and their reps – at the London wholesale markets.

At the hearing John Hendy QC accused Smith, allegedly a devout Mormon, of lying under oath. In November the Tribunal handed down its verdict; the strikers had been unfairly dismissed. At a meeting in Caernarfon between the union, its solicitors and Smith, called to negotiate a settlement and return to work, Smith, either for real or contrived reasons, lost his temper and stormed out of the meeting. He was subsequently heard on BBC radio saying that he would appeal the decision of the Tribunal and that the firm was running out of money to pay any awards the courts may make.

The picketing continued into the new year, with another Christmas delivery from the London wholesale markets. Smith put Friction Dynamics into administration in August 2003, so never carried out his threat to take an appeal to the Employment Appeal Tribunal. The union returned to the Employment Tribunal in April 2004 – a remedies hearing to seek the payment of compensation for being unfairly dismissed. Eventually the basic award of £5,200 per person was paid from public funds.

But the key point was that, although the members eventually won through at the Employment Tribunal, the employer had closed down

19 Pritchard & Edwards, *On the Line*, p.41.

Friction Dynamics and restarted production under the name Dynamex Friction. Friction Dynamics had debts of £8 million so there was no money to pay workers compensation even though the same plant was producing the same product for the same customers but under a different name.

There are two enduring legal features of the Friction Dynamics dispute that need addressing even today.

First, 'the most important reform to the law in recognition of this case would be the suspension of the contract of employment during strike action. Already established in other EU countries, such a law would constitute a positive step towards the UK fulfilling its international obligations on human rights'.[20]

And second, as John Hendy QC argued at the time:

> we have to get rid of the ban on secondary picketing. If that were the case the T&G would have able to ask their other members to officially support the Friction lads. They could have asked the lorry drivers not to transport Friction Dynamics parts. They could have asked their workers in the car factories not to handle Friction Dynamics parts ... That would have had quite an impact, and certainly the dispute wouldn't have lasted half as long as a result.[21]

Human Resource Management

John Fisher

At the same time as the shock doctrine of deindustrialisation and an oppressive legal regime were being implemented, some employers, particularly in motor manufacture and petrochemicals, tried a different approach – to wean their workforce away from an independent voice at work, expressed through their union, to an altogether more class collaborationist approach known variously, and almost interchangeably, as human resources management (HRM) or total quality management (TQM).

Motor manufacture was the first to try these new methods, as it was fear of Japanese competition in the product market that led employers to seek to emulate Japanese management methods, known as *kanban*, in British factories.

In the union's industrial work, the growth of HRM was the major issue of the 1980s and 1990s. Management consultants were proposing

---

20 B. Davies, *The Right to Strike: Has the Law Moved on Since the Friction Dynamics Dispute?* (IER Briefing, 2009), p.4.
21 Quoted in Pritchard & Edwards, *On the Line*, p.125.

fundamental changes in working practices, including teamworking, continuous improvement, lean production, customer first, outsourcing and TQM. The initial reaction of the union was curiosity, followed by opposition, then by a more sophisticated response of 'constructive engagement' later in the decade. The union's education programme was to play a key role in the evolution of the union's response to HRM.[22]

T&G members in the Automotive Trade Group began to take note of the 'Quality Movement' in the early 1980s. At both Vauxhall and Ford the company started to promote the new techniques, followed by companies in other sectors.

At this stage, there was concern that these new techniques represented a broad-based attack on worker solidarity:

> HRM consists of three interlocking elements, all affecting the trade union role. First, the introduction of new ideological concepts into industrial relations, the essence of which is to increase the identification of the workforce with the goals of the company or organisation. Chief amongst these are 'quality', 'customer first', 'right first time', 'world class', and other corporatist concepts. These values are usually disseminated through a 'mission statement' which identifies the ideological terms of reference for present and future activity in terms agreeable to the employer, and marginalises non-incorporated goals and organisations. These management techniques ... seek to fill the ideological vacuum with a host of ideas centred around bringing workers on board with the organisation's competitiveness problem, and incorporating workers into the company's goals'.[23]

In September 1984 the Automotive Trade Group requested the GEC to issue guidelines to active members, shop stewards and officers. As a result, the GEC issued a warning of the dangers of so-called Employee Involvement and Quality Circle schemes; on the basis that:

- they should not be introduced without union scrutiny and consent;

- representatives should be chosen in line with union representative machinery;

---

22 For the general experience of the union with HRM see J. Fisher, 'The trade union response to HRM in the UK: the case of the TGWU', *Human Resource Management Journal*, 1995, vol.5, no.3, pp.7–23.
23 J. Fisher, B. Camfield & A. Weir, 'New Management Techniques: back to basics for the unions?', *Communist Review*, 1994, November.

- where they exist, such schemes should be brought in line with union structures and under union control;

- in no case should they be allowed to undermine union structures or collective bargaining.

The Research Department was asked to draw up a booklet drawing attention to the dangers of employee involvement and quality circles being introduced without the control of the union.[24] This booklet was issued in July 1985 incorporating these views. However, this initial 'oppositional' position was difficult to sustain in the light of the pervasiveness and sophistication of HRM techniques. Also, many members and particular sections of the union felt the techniques actually constituted an improvement in industrial relations. Teamworking and employee involvement were popular.

In September 1987 a book was written by Tony Woodley, then a district officer but formerly the convenor of Vauxhall's Ellesmere Port factory, later to become the National Secretary of the Automotive Trade Group, and General Secretary of the union. This document provided a more sophisticated analysis of quality circles and teamworking – under the label quality of working life (QWL) – than had been seen in the union up to that point, and stressed the importance of an educational response to the problem.

Woodley argued:

[I]n its initial stages, at least, QWL is often popular with a portion of the rank-and-file. If the union seeks withdrawal it may force a rebellion from QWL enthusiasts who will then be drawn even more towards a company viewpoint. Local union leaders must educate members to the hidden traps and pitfalls of QWL. The second alternative is to make QWL work for the unions:

1. The union must develop its own goals and strategies before it enters 'joint' activities.
2. Union leadership at all levels must be united.
3. The union should do its own long-range planning.
4. The union should seek independent help and expert advice when determining the union's goals and training for QWL.
5. The union has to be prepared for hard bargaining to protect its interests in QWL.[25]

---

24 General Executive Council Minutes, 5 December 1994, Minute 987, p.229.
25 T. Woodley, *Quality of Working Life – Quality Circles* (T&G, 1987).

This opened up a more complex and sophisticated approach to HRM, and also the central role of education in meeting the new challenge.

The union's Chemical, Oil and Rubber Trade Group, led by Fred Higgs, was also involved, having suffered derecognition during the 1980s in companies such as Norsk Hydro on Humberside, and in Shell.

In September 1991, the National Committee of the Trade Group submitted a motion to the GEC along the following lines: that this is one of the most important industrial issues the union is currently facing with the potential of such management techniques severely undermining and removing trade union membership within many companies, and requests that the union provides a series of courses on the subject.

As a result, an HRM working party was set up under the auspices of Deputy General Secretary Jack Adams to examine the whole question of management techniques and derecognition. From 1991 the approach of the union took on a more sophisticated and complex character, as the subtlety of the new techniques became better understood. This became the dominant element in the evolution of the union's policy of 'constructive engagement' through the 1990s, and underpinned the exponential growth in joint training courses with employers.

An important example of this new approach was a seminar, 'Works Councils and the Management of Change', held at Eastbourne in December 1992, with over 120 delegates from automotive plants in France, Germany, Spain, Italy, Ireland and Belgium. The seminar was financed from the EU fund established to prepare the way for European Works Councils. Speakers included Dave Robertson from the Canadian Autoworkers' Union, Jack Adams, Tony Woodley, John Fisher, senior managers from Vauxhall and Rover, and Peter Wickens from Nissan, an arch-advocate of TQM.

In November 1994, a major event, a motor industry components conference, was held at the Birmingham NEC. It was primarily organised by Tony Woodley and Joe Irvin. Much work was undertaken in Rover, around the *Rover Tomorrow* agreement, which was concluded in 1992. Jack Adams was involved in this, and it was accepted that *Rover Tomorrow* would be an enabling agreement. This was accepted by the union as the basis for 'positive engagement' as a response to TQM/HRM.

These events formed the background to a later resolution – Composite 5 – to the 1993 BDC, which included a definition of 'positive engagement'. This now became the union's policy: 'Conference states that education and training about lean production and TQM cannot therefore maintain a simple oppositionist stance. We must seek to develop a strategy of positive engagement with the employers on the above whilst at the same time retaining the trust and support of the membership'.[26]

26 Minutes of the Proceedings of the 35th Biennial Delegate Conference 1993,

In 1995 the union produced a booklet *Change at Work*. Regular 'Change at Work' courses, tutored by Les Ford, were established for delegates from the trade groups and also for individual companies such as ICI, BOC, Cadbury and Unilever. In the public sector, courses on HRM in the Health Service and British Waterways were held in 1996 and 1997. The subject was integrated into all regional education programmes. Joint training with employers and company-specific courses also became an established part of the programme. But normally all the areas covered in the curriculum had to be mutually agreed, thus keeping the union centre-stage.

It is, however, debateable whether the union benefitted from this policy of 'constructive engagement'. Where the company remained organised, the new working arrangements probably did little harm, and some companies like Nissan were organised in this way right from the start. However, the experience at Rover showed that if the company was running down or facing closure or takeover, then 'positive engagement' was trumped by threats or actual closure, and if a company was determined to deunionise then the battle for survival reverted to much more traditional methods. As always, the big question would be 'how much have the workers benefited' from the resultant large increases in productivity?

Summary

Without any shadow of doubt, the anti-union laws passed by Conservative governments under Margaret Thatcher and John Major had a debilitating impact on the organisation of industrial action, which of course was the intention. The new legal regime brought about the precipitous decline in the coverage of collective bargaining, which was, as a percentage of the labour force, greater than union membership density. The collapse of collective bargaining is a major cause in the long-term decline in the share of GDP going to wages and salaries; in other word workers were really getting poorer in this period.

In the case of the Liverpool docks the shop-floor organisation led by the shop stewards kept the dispute going for an amazing length of time, one highlight being the level of support mobilised particularly from the community, most particularly women supporters and, at the macro level, the degree of international support from dock workers and their unions overseas.

However, their action started as a spontaneous walkout organised without a ballot of the membership and all the associated procedures demanded by the anti-union laws. If the union had endorsed the dispute

– made it official – it ran the risk of court action, effectively being sued for damages by the employers and possible sequestration of the union's assets. It was on this point that the General Secretary argued against declaring the action official on the grounds that he was protecting the fabric of the union.

The new laws had clearly worked as intended.

In the Friction Dynamics dispute the cautious hand of the local full-time official ensured that all the balloting requirements were complied with, so the dispute remained within the strictures imposed by the Thatcher laws. So far so good. But what the Friction Dynamics workers really needed to successfully prosecute the dispute was for the workers in the car companies supplied with Friction Dynamic brake linings to be able to boycott these products, leading to, it would be supposed, either pressure from the car manufacturers on Friction Dynamics to satisfactorily resolve the dispute or market pressure on Friction Dynamics as the car manufacturers turned to alternative suppliers.

No amount of balloting, or giving the employer notice, could have made such action by workers in the car plants lawful. For the Friction Dynamics workers to have picketed the car plants calling on car workers to take the boycott action, so-called secondary picketing, would have opened up the union to be sued for damages and possible sequestration – back to the Liverpool docks conundrum.

Again, the new laws had clearly worked as intended.

The BA cabin crew dispute was not particularly impeded by the anti-union laws, although it has been noted that BA management threatened court action for breach of contract for any crew who went on strike.

Aspects of these three disputes showed that more was required than a simple repeal of the Tory anti-union laws, a call that was gaining currency at that time. A comprehensive reform of trade union law and rights at work was becoming essential, including the repeal of the anti-union laws and more – for example, suspension of the employment contract during industrial action and mechanisms to enforce awards made at the Employment Tribunal.

Many in the union leaderships, including Bill Morris and his executive officers, were hoping that an incoming Labour government would resolve the problem. But, as we shall see, that was furthest from Tony Blair's list of policy priorities.

In conclusion, BA's *Putting People First* was part of a new approach aimed at winning the hearts and minds of staff, to identify with corporate goals, the logical extension of which would be to portray the union as an unnecessary third party in the employment relationship. Before that stage could be reached, however, Ayling announced a massive programme of cuts, which led to the 1997 cabin crew strike.

The new HRM/TQM regimes were mainly seen as a manufacturing phenomenon, as shown by the lead taken in policy development by members in car manufacture and petrochemicals. However, the cabin crew dispute could have been used more widely by the T&G to show that HRM/TQM, and other aspects of the new management techniques that employers were using to facilitate a corporate friendly culture change, was a chimera and was exposed as such when corporate strategy switched back to an aggressive right to manage.

3

Organise or Die

The Turn to Organising

The T&G became the preeminent advocate of organising unions in the last decade of the twentieth century and into the twenty-first century. Why was that so?

Trade unions in the UK and across the industrialised world had been losing membership on a massive scale from 1980 onwards. And this had impacted heavily on the T&G. Organised jobs in manufacturing and transport had been shrinking fast as a result of the industrial restructuring that was being promoted by the Thatcher government. Manufacturing jobs contracted by over 15 per cent in just three years and unemployment soared to over three million in the early 1980s.

Membership in the T&G had reached its peak, with over two million members in 1979 at the beginning of the Thatcher period. By 1992 membership stood at around half that figure (1,080,638) – down again to some 800,000 by 2003. Small wonder then that the situation was causing concern. The minutes of the GEC from the early 1990s document the problems that these continuing losses were causing, not least their dire financial consequences.

So how to respond? There were efforts to increase membership through mergers with other trade unions (see Chapter 6). There were attempts to cut back on costs and reorganise T&G structures (see Chapter 1). And there was a more general sense of retrenchment emanating from the top under Bill Morris' leadership as General Secretary. The emphasis was on preserving the fabric of the union; in other words being prudent, avoiding risks in the context of the financial penalties that were associated with breaches of anti-trade union legislation. This was about keeping one's powder dry, striving to defend the status quo and opting for partnership working, all of this in the context of New Labour under the leadership of Tony Blair from 1994.

Almost as soon as he was elected General Secretary, Bill Morris engaged a firm of US management consultants, with alleged labour movement links, Klein & Co, to work on restructuring the union.

But internal restructuring could not be the only response to the crisis facing the T&G in the early years of the neo-liberal assault. Industrial restructuring, major defeats inflicted on the working class praetorian guard – miners, dockers, printers – and a legal shackling of the traditional forms of trade union activity meant that there had to be a new approach to building the unions of the future. There was a turn to organising, although the move in this new direction was very unevenly paced.

Morris, as Deputy General Secretary, had already launched the 'Link Up' campaign in 1987, with the specific aim of recruiting those working in what came to be called the peripheral labour market – temporary and part-time workers, and very often women. On the one hand this initiative could be chalked up as a success, as it raised the recruitment rate to over 200,000 new members a year. In reality this was like trying to fill a leaky bucket; the increased rate of joining hardly kept up with membership losses resulting from redundancies and closures that were an essential part of neo-liberal industrial restructuring.

Region 1 launched its own campaign. Barry Camfield, when he became Regional Organiser, had launched the regional 1-2-1 campaign that encouraged union members to try to recruit a non-member to the union. These Region 1 initiatives really gathered pace and were more in line with the emerging turn to organising, when Camfield became Regional Secretary and Ken Fuller was appointed Regional Organiser.

Region 6 also ran its own initiative in the 1980s aimed particularly at contract cleaners on Merseyside. In a move very prescient of what would come to be called community organising, the T&G declared a minimum wage rate for contract cleaners and then set about creating havoc outside the targeted building with not just the cleaners demonstrating but their families and others from the community. The intention was to cause so much inconvenience that the building's occupier or owner, whoever let the cleaning contract, would pressure the cleaning company to pay the union declared rate of pay.

Len McCluskey recalls in his memoirs:

[T]rying to organise contract cleaners ... It was difficult – they were in a precarious position. But they had a brilliant union officer helping them ... called John Farrell. He set a Merseyside-wide minimum rate of pay and demanded that contractors meet it. They would tell him to get lost, so he would organise demonstrations outside the offices cleaned by the women (they were all women) and get everyone and anyone to come and assist in their struggle ... John handled 54 disputes in a 12-month period and won every one, establishing an unofficial minimum wage for cleaners on Merseyside.[1]

---

1 L. McCluskey, *Always Red* (OR Books, 2021), p.293.

The Emerging Influence of the US Unions

Barry Camfield (interview, 23 June 2020)

One of the key influences had been John Sweeney, then president of the US SEIU. He had been developing approaches based on the power of members acting for themselves. It wasn't enough to simply recruit members with high expectations that couldn't be fulfilled unless the workers themselves were actively engaged. And members had to be recruited in new ways in any case, to take account of the threats to trade union organising at the time.

For example, organising Eurotunnel workers. A team had tried to recruit the workers who were the operating staff at Eurotunnel by standing outside the workplace. But this didn't work, as people felt too exposed by being seen talking to trade union organisers. So, people were contacted by letter, followed up by door knocking to speak to people in the safety of their homes. A T&G ex-branch secretary was identified in the process and he became the contact point, recruiting others. He became the branch secretary when the Eurotunnel branch was established in 1994.

These illustrations of regional autonomy are examples of what was then commonplace in the T&G. Len McCluskey, in interview, made the point that even though Ron Todd had established the National Co-ordinating Committee, chaired at one point by Barry Camfield, which brought together all 11 regional organisers, regional autonomy was rife. In McCluskey's view there was a need for national direction, which meant a challenge to the hegemony of the regional secretaries.

Although the union nationally was promoting its 'Link Up' campaign and Regions 1 and 6 were also trying to adapt to the new circumstances, to properly understand the turn to organising we must firstly look to unions elsewhere in the world.

The Neo-Liberal Counter-Revolution

In the period after the Second World War, and the subsequent long boom, governments in the West had a relatively benign view of trade unions, often as part of a strategy for showing that socialism, or at least Soviet-style communism, was not the only game in town; that workers could in fact prosper under capitalism, with no need to veer to the left.

As the 1970s opened it was clear that there was change afoot. In the UK, the Conservatives tried to limit the powers of the unions through their Industrial Relations Act, more fully dealt with in earlier volumes. It was in

Chile that the world was first exposed to the new economic thinking when, following a bloody coup in 1973 against the left government of Salvador Allende, the *golpista* military government, advised by graduates of the University of Chicago Economics Department, embarked on a process of public spending cuts and privatisation that we now recognise as part of the neo-liberal playbook.

The election in 1979 of Margaret Thatcher as UK Prime Minster and Ronald Reagan as US President in 1980 marked the end of the Keynesian post-war settlement and ushered in neo-liberalism and the rise of the corporation and the super-rich as the new world order. This was a process greatly enhanced by the collapse of the Soviet Union in 1991; now the neo-liberals really could say that 'there was no alternative'.[2]

Public spending cuts, industrial restructuring away from base metals and manufacturing and government-encouraged employer hostility saw US unions lose 20 per cent of their members who worked in the private sector during the first part of the 1980s. In the UK, TUC unions never again achieved such membership levels as those in 1979/1980, with some 13 million members covering over half the labour force; as in the US, the biggest losses were in the private sector.

The US Unions, New Ideas about Organising and First Landfall in Australia

During the long boom it has been argued that unions had shifted from being militant *organisers of* workers to effectively becoming an outside agency that provided a *service to* workers in their dealings with employers, either individually on grievance or disciplinary handling or collectively with bargaining new agreements or contracts. In other words, rather than acting *with* workers unions were acting *for* workers.

The progressive prescription put forward to arrest the precipitous decline in membership and to renew the militant spirit of trade unionism was that unions needed to change from being locked into the servicing model and had to undergo rapid cultural change, to become organising unions. The contrasting features of each model are set out in the table devised by the Australian unions' education and training provider.

---

2 For a discussion of the Soviet Union being seen as a good example, see E. Hobsbawm, 'Goodbye to all That', *Marxism Today*, October 1990; and I. Sinclair, 'How communism improved the lot of workers in the West and saved capitalism', *Morning Star*, 23 March 2022.

Table 1: Contrasting the Servicing Model with the Organising Model

Servicing Union	Organising Union
The union is seen as a third party; it enters the workplace to increase membership or solve problems	Members own the campaign to unionise their workplace
Unions tell members how they can solve their problems	Members generate their own issues and organise to solve them together
Relying on the employer to provide lists of names of workers to union official	Mapping the workplace and staff attitudes are crucial – names and information are provided by the workers
Relying on workplace access and employer co-operation	Initial organising can be done outside work – in workers' homes and other places
Cold selling union membership by organisers	Establishing initial contacts and finding natural leaders to help recruit
Selling the union for services and insurance protection	Workers empowered to do it for themselves through education and support
Relying on full-time officials to recruit and solve problems	An internal organising committee formed, and workers encouraged to build the union through one-to-one organising
Recruitment is seen as a separate activity	Recruitment and organising are integrated
Results are achieved but they are likely to be short term	Results are obtained through sustained efforts – more likely to be permanent
The union is blamed when it cannot get results	Members share decisions and solve problems together with union leaders
Members complain they pay fees, and the union does nothing	Members make a real contribution to union struggles and identify with the union; an attack on the union is an attack on them
Organisers resent members for not coming to meetings or participating	The image of the union is positive and active
Management acts, while the union reacts, and it is always on the defensive	The union has its own agenda with members involved and it keeps management off balance

Source: Trade Union Training Authority (Australia).

It was in the US that it became clear that a new approach was needed. So in 1989 the American Federation of Labor–Congress of Industrial Organisations (AFL-CIO) launched the Organising Institute, 'an in-house academy that trained students and rank and filers in the ABCs of organising'.[3] In 1995 an insurgent group of unions, campaigning as 'New Voice', drew up a slate to challenge the existing AFL-CIO leadership – John Sweeney of the Service Employees International Union (SEIU) for President, the Mineworkers' Richard Trumka for Secretary-Treasurer and the municipal workers' Linda Chavez-Thompson for a yet to be created position of Executive Vice-President.

Sweeney promised to devote one-third of the federation's resources to organising as well as redefining the federation's political work should New Voice win. When Sweeney became President he moved more and more resources into union organising.

Success, as the old saying goes, has many parents. So it was with the transformative adoption by some T&G leaders of the organising model. It has been noted previously that Barry Camfield was greatly influenced by John Sweeney and used the new approach to organising in the Eurotunnel campaign that came to fruition in 1994.

Len McCluskey recalls being similarly impressed by Andy Stern:

[A]t a conference in New York in 1992 I heard a speech by Andy Stern, leader of the American union SEIU, about a method of organising based on empowering the workers on the shop floor. I was inspired. I became a champion of that organising ethos and later encouraged Tony Woodley to embrace it. Under his leadership – largely thanks to his bravery and willingness to try something new – we were able to set up an organising department that has since become an integral part of Unite.[4]

It was remarkable that the recommendations for change for the T&G put forward by the Bill Morris-commissioned US management consultants, Klein & Co, was very light on organising. Klein & Co came with an alleged reputation of assisting unions in the US with restructuring projects. But at the very time Klein & Co were advising the T&G, the biggest change in the US unions was the turn to organising, about which Klein & Co had little, if anything, to say.

There is just a single paragraph, under the heading 'Recruitment', in the booklet known as the *Klein Report*:

---

3 H. Meyerson, 'A second chance: the new AFL-CIO and the prospective revival of American labor', in Mort J-A (ed.), *Not Your Father's Union Movement: Inside the AFL-CIO* (Verso, 1998), p.10.

4 McCluskey, *Always Red*, p.300.

[T]he recruitment and organisation of new members is a job which is the responsibility of every member, lay committee and full-time officer, in particular the regional organisers and the National Co-ordinating Committee. Klein was able to show us the level of resources currently allocated to organising and, as with every other matter, it is up to the union to determine what, if any, changes are necessary. The GEC has authorised a variety of imaginative campaigns including *Link Up* and *One-to-One*, which have been developed in the regions and trade groups. Approximately 250,000 new members join the T&G each year, this represents a turnover of 20% per annum. We need this number, and more, just to stand still. But as we are currently losing members, the union has had to consider membership retention strategies as well as recruitment strategies. The use of direct debit is considered useful in this field.[5]

Clearly, what was being recommended to the T&G was not cutting edge in the US. However, before the diffusion of the AFL-CIO New Voice model on organising was eventually picked up in Britain it firstly reached Australia.

In Australia also, the turn to organising was associated with an insurgent new leadership; this was marked by the accession of Greg Combet as Secretary of the Australian Council of Trade Unions (ACTU). This,

reignited the debate about organising that had begun earlier in the decade, emphasising the building of workplace activism, organising non-union workers, making better and more efficient use of technology and management techniques and broadening the agenda beyond the workplace ... [and] signalled a deeper and practical commitment to organising unionism on the part of the leadership of the union movement, a stance reinforced at the ACTU's policy making Congress 2000.[6]

5 T&G, *One Union T&G. Recommendations of Klein & Co 'Report' to Members* (T&G, 1992), p.20.

6 B. Carter & R. Cooper, 'The organising model and the management of change', *Relations Industrielles/Industrial Relations*, 2002, vol.57, no.4, p.727.

The T&G's Past Experiences of Organising

The T&G's legacy has already been cited as a source of inspiration for contemporary times. The union was built on the basis of trade union struggles from the 1889 Great Dock Strike onwards. Jack Jones has also been quoted as a more recent role model for trade union organisers to follow. In his autobiography, Jack Jones described the approach that he had been developing in Coventry, applying this in his work as Engineering Group Secretary for the whole of the Midlands region of the union. Membership had been small and scattered over a range of firms in parts of the West Midlands, so recruitment had been essential in order to strengthen the union's negotiating strength. He explained to those officials who were less than enthusiastic about organising (described as relishing 'the friendship of managers and personnel officers' and 'happy to enjoy the fruits of office without working for them' – that 'they were like generals without an army'. They needed to earn their title to leadership by showing that they could organise.[7]

Leading by example, Jack Jones produced a range of recruitment materials. Then, using what contacts he could, he arranged meetings in pubs and clubs near the factories. Often the best results were obtained 'by small gatherings in people's homes', he explained.[8] This was about building support by engaging with workers through those that they trusted, in situations where they felt safe and confident enough to share their concerns.

Jack Jones was not only concerned with recruitment numbers though, important though this was, in terms of strengthening the union's bargaining position. He was also deeply committed to building democratic decision-making within the union. Trade union officials were servants of their members, he explained to a manager who expected officials to get their members back to work. 'I knew that we would never build strong unions while such attitudes prevailed'.[9]

On the contrary, in his view, the workers themselves should be the ones to make such decisions. This was about deep organising for empower-ment, in other words prefiguring the models that were to be promoted subsequently, as part of organising agendas within the T&G. This was the legacy that has been shaping organising agendas ever since in the T&G. The rebuilding of union membership and union organisation in the London docks at Tilbury after the defeat of abolition of the National Dock Labour Scheme was just such an example.

---

7 J. Jones, *Union Man: an Autobiography* (Collins, 1986), p.140.
8 Jones, *Union Man*, p.140.
9 Jones, *Union Man*, p.142.

Rebuilding Organisation in the London Docks — Health and Safety Is the Key

Andy Green (interview, 14 July 2020)

When Andy Green started work in Tilbury as a young man in his 20s in late 1989, there had been an atmosphere of fear. The National Dock Labour Scheme had been abolished and 17 shop stewards had been sacked that summer. The aim had been to break the trade union and make sure that there would be no trade union presence in future. New workers were recruited in groups, 30 at a time, as part of this bid for control. 'We were told we were to be a new breed ... We weren't to be tainted with the old ways'. Almost everyone in the area did actually have a family member with connections with the docks, though; they just kept quiet about it. So, this attempt to ban anyone with docks connections was unrealistic, as it turned out, a mistake on the employers' part.

The employers treated the workforce in degrading ways, with contempt in fact, just as they had treated the previous workforce before them. So, this soon led to the same resentments, especially when it came to health and safety issues. Dock work is very dangerous, so health and safety is literally a matter of life and death.

Andy Green (Unite convenor at Tilbury, Unite EC member for Docks & Rails and Chair of Unite Executive Council) became involved in organising around precisely such concerns. He and another docker went to a branch meeting to seek advice from former dockers about how to tackle the problems. These former dockers were very supportive, telling them how it ought to be in terms of their rights, explaining the law on health and safety. Far from resenting these newcomers for effectively taking over their jobs, they were really very helpful indeed.

Andy Green and his colleagues soon realised that they needed to build up the union membership if they were to challenge the employers on these issues effectively. 'This was easier said than done'.

People were still frightened back then (there was an atmosphere of fear even among those with a background of union membership), because there was so much intimidation from the employers. Ironically, though, it was the employers themselves who actually helped to build the recruitment process, because they were so very nasty. As a result, workers began to listen to the argument that this was not right — that it was time for some pushback.

Andy and others would meet informally, in canteens and off the quayside in tearooms. And there, in these meetings, they began to plan unofficial actions, such as slow downs on the ships and bans on weekend overtime, as protests. Slowly, slowly, through taking these types of actions over immediate grievances and winning small gains, solidarity was built up, as confidence developed.

There was a very strong trade union culture here – despite the levels of fear that had been inculcated. This pride in the union was fostered in a number of ways. This was about showing that trade union membership was building up. The question was not 'why don't you join the union' but 'why aren't you a union member'. Being a union member was to be seen as the norm. Non-members were coming to feel that they were they the outsiders. And exaggerated claims of 90 per cent union membership were put about – which alarmed the employers (even if the actual figure was maybe closer to 30 per cent)!

Health and safety issues were the key issues on which to mobilise the workforce. As has already been explained, docks were – and still are – very dangerous workplaces, with serious accidents and fatalities. Management were susceptible to pressure on these concerns. Activists built up connections with engineering staff who would (secretly) pass on documents such as maintenance records, showing activists when equipment was dangerous because it was not being properly maintained. Activists would then confront the bosses with these failings and demand action as a result. Management could see that these activists really knew what they were talking about. And they could understand that these were very serious issues.

These discussions (about health and safety) could be confrontational. The employers had to listen because they needed to get the ships turned around fast. And dock workers could control the pace of work through tactics such as overtime bans and slow-downs. This all gave them confidence, going from strength to strength as they made each gain, including very practical gains such as getting double time for overtime working (which had been the norm, previously).

Andy Green spoke of the traditional pride in being a dock worker and a proud member of the union. At Tilbury this pride was re-enforced in a number of ways, demonstrating their identity and pride in the job. LE/10 branch was Ben Tillett's old branch. The office was decorated with black and white pictures of past struggles from the 1889 Dock Strike onwards. Learning about the history of the union added to this sense of identity and pride. Andy Green subsequently explained that Keith Watson, the full time official, had told them about more recent aspects of the T&G's history too, including the strikes that had taken place even during the Second World War. Keith Watson had been very helpful in terms of helping them to take a structured approach to organising. This had been very supportive – a good example of organising agendas being provided with effective back-up support from the relevant officials.

Summarising the lessons, Andy Green emphasised the importance of this trade union culture, making it much easier to organise than it would have been on a green field site. In addition, it had been important to build up confidence through taking up immediate issues and winning gains, making real improvements in the process. The union had also been supportive to members and their families, taking up their cases and recruiting them into the branch if they had problems (such as claims for an industrial injury), providing information and advice. This made more work for the branch, but was very much appreciated by those concerned. It was this whole approach that enabled the T&G to go from strength to strength.

Bringing the US and Other Experiences to Britain

From the AFL-CIO and ACTU experiences it is clear that the adoption of the trappings of an organising model without the commitment of a leadership prepared to initiate and support the necessary culture change is unlikely to succeed, which is why the New Voice and Combet insurgency were the key drivers that moved the organising agenda forwards.

By the 1990s, the TUC was looking to learn from international experience, identifying strategies for tackling the problems associated with declining trade union membership. US approaches were seen as particularly relevant in this context. One of the most significant of these recruitment initiatives came from the SEIU under the leadership of Andy Stern. At that time, back in the late 1990s, the TUC was interested in developing strategies to replicate the SEIU's remarkable recruitment successes under Stern's leadership.

When John Monks was elected General Secretary of the TUC in 1993, he abolished much of the old bureaucratic committee structure that reflected industries that were fast disappearing and moved the operation of Congress House to issue-based task groups. One of these groups was the New Unionism project, chaired by Deputy General Secretary Tony Burke (who retired as Unite Assistant General Secretary) of the Graphical, Paper & Media Union (GPMU), a Unite legacy union.

New unionism may be explained as follows:

[I]n September 1997, John Monks ... set out his vision of 'new' unionism to the first TUC conference to be held under a Labour Government for 19 years. ... Mr Monks highlighted that this needed 'new' thinking, 'new' action and 'new' unionism. He said that unions should be looking at new ways of recruitment and commitment, so that young people can begin to build a safe future at work ... To the employers, Mr Monks said that the TUC would be pushing for a new way forward which would include partnership, long-term invest-ment and employment security. He said that the unions realised that employers need maximum flexibility in order to compete, and that the TUC supported this but wanted a positive flexibility which gets rid of the old 'hire-and-fire brigade' of employers.[10]

10   https://www.eurofound.europa.eu/publications/article/1997/john-monks-outlines-new-unionism.

According to Burke, in interview, the GPMU had recognised in the early 1990s that industrial restructuring and technological development could destroy the traditional membership base of the union. A GPMU delegation went to the US to meet the International Graphical Union (now part of the Teamsters) initially to look at how information technology may assist with member contact and mobilisation. During this visit they were introduced to an AFL-CIO mentor-organiser who explained to them the new approach to organising. The union again returned to the US to take part in the AFL-CIO's Union Summer, in Cleveland, an annual training and assessment centre used to spot likely organisers among sympathetic college students and young union activists.

The GPMU was learning at first hand the practice of strategic campaigning; a positive outcome of these contacts with the US unions was that it attempted to put on its own version of Union Summer, but for full-time officers, based in Stoke-on-Trent. Further, the GPMU conference was one to switch resources from servicing to organising; the union appointed new people to the staff of the union with specific responsibility for organising.

Given that the GPMU seemed to be ahead of the curve, Burke was an obvious choice in 1996 to chair the New Unionism task group and, subsequently, the management of the Organising Academy. Frances O'Grady, recently retired TUC General Secretary (and sometime previously with the T&G Research Department), was appointed as Head of the Organising Academy. Drawing on the American and Australian experience, the TUC opened its Organising Academy in January 1998, with the specific objective of training organisers and making a change in the culture of unions, a change that would, or should, be the turn to organising.

The Organising Academy had an intake of 36 trainee organisers in its first year. The TUC was looking to recruit young activists, especially women and Black, Asian and Ethnic Minority (BAEM) members, based on the view that 'like recruits like' (although in practice there were not so many of the latter). The aim was to develop a cadre of organisers from different trade unions, sharing experiences and providing each other with mutual support, both on the course and subsequently, when working as organisers in their respective unions. This had been an important dimension of the whole approach, enabling the organisers to develop networks for the future, building a movement in other words.

The course itself offered a combination of theoretical input, organisational skills and political skills, (provided at the TUC College, then in Crouch End, London). Trainee organisers also gained practical experiences, each trainee working within a specific trade union as part of their course.

Sam Gurney's views are mirrored in the findings of an academic study, evaluating the achievements of the TUC's Organising Academy, as

The TUC Organising Academy

Sam Gurney (interview, 12 June 2020)

One of the first cohort of trainee organisers, Sam Gurney (now the TUC Regional Secretary for the London, South East & Eastern Region) recounted his experiences and the lessons that he had taken from this.

Sam had been assigned to the Society of Telecom Executives (STE, now part of the Prospect union) organising white-collar workers in telecoms. The union was developing innovative approaches at the time, addressing the changes that were taking place in the telecoms sector, developing approaches to organising freelance workers. So, he found that this was a valuable placement, providing learning about ways of developing innovative strategies for the future.

Sam was also very positive about his learning from the T&G's experiences and approaches. The T&G had not sent members onto the first year's course (although Sharon Graham, who subsequently became T&G's Director of Organising and subsequently Unite General Secretary, did attend, but on her own initiative). But T&G approaches and experiences were centrally significant all the same. T&G trainers came in to provide direct inputs to the course, including inputs based upon the T&G's histories of organising from dock workers in the nineteenth century through to more recent times, including Jack Jones' own work organising the unorganised in the Midlands. He had taken these lessons – and his contacts from the course – with him when he went on to work for another trade union subsequently.

Sam went on to explain that he had also collaborated with T&G officers and organisers, subsequently (when he was working at the General, Municipal and Boilermakers Union (GMB)), when they were organising casino workers, and then again, later on, when they were organising hotel and catering workers. These officials and organisers had been absolutely committed to building membership and to getting unorganised people into membership, he reflected. And they had been prepared to collaborate with others in order to do so most effectively. The encouragement to collaborate across trade unions had been a particularly valuable feature of the TUC course overall, in fact. It was sad, in his view, that trade unions had tended to revert to a more trade union-specific approach, in more recent times.

There had been significant achievements overall from the TUC's Organising Academy, Sam concluded. The organising agenda had been essential to respond to declining trade union membership, inculcating the attitude that you had to start from where people were, with workplace-based discussions, focusing on people's issues. This approach had been part of a wider shift in the balance between the servicing and the organising roles for trade unions. Trade unions had been holding their own in terms of membership, as a result, despite the difficulties of the wider socio-economic and political context. More women members were being recruited too, and both officials and reps were looking more like the workforces that they were representing (including younger women and BAEM members). These changes were all the more significant given that there had in the past been resistance to the organising approach in some quarters in the trade union movement.

There were continuing challenges, however. While it was relatively straight-forward to recruit in areas where there were already members, it was much harder to recruit in unorganised, green field areas. Precarious employment added to these problems for organisers; this was resource-intensive work. So there needed to be continuing support right from the top – which had been the case with T&G/Unite in his view.

the project had developed and changed over the ten-year period from its inception.[11]

The T&G, much to the TUC's disappointment did not participate in the Academy; but this reluctance, as we shall see, was not from a conservative, no-change position. The TUC was hopeful that the Academy would be a means to break into private sector services; it was in the private sector that union membership losses had been the greatest and which showed the greatest growth in employment; the T&G would have been a gateway into this sector.

The Development of the T&G Turn to Organising

The election of the Conservatives under Thatcher in 1979 and the government's attack on the trade union movement had been part of a predetermined strategy, as shown with the government's preparations to take on the miners, in the lead up to the Miner's Strike of 1984–1985. It was paradoxical that the T&G had seemed so big at the time, with over two million members. But this strength in numbers was only part of the picture. As Barry Camfield, who became Regional Organiser in Region 1 in 1986, explained: 'we seemed unprepared to tackle it' (that is, unprepared to tackle the challenges of the Thatcher era, of neo-liberalism). So, unions had to start thinking afresh. The old servicing model was not enough. A new organising approach was required. This needed to be based on the power of members acting for themselves.

11 M. Simms, J. Holgate & E. Heery, *Union Voices: Tactics and Tensions in UK Organising* (Cornell University Press, 2013).

There had been battles of ideas to be won too, though. Not everyone was convinced of the case for organising. There were full-time officers who were reluctant to change. It was challenging to organise workers in unorganised workplaces, especially if they were locked into precarious employment. And there were issues to be addressed in terms of tackling discrimination and building solidarity. There had been reps who were dubious about organising migrant workers, for example, seeing them as potentially undermining pay and conditions, rather than seeing the need for solidarity to prevent one section of the workforce from being used against another section.

There were continuing debates about priorities. Was the focus to be on organising workers in precarious jobs, as compared with the focus on more strategic sectoral priorities – or both?

From the mid-1990s the union's conference was increasingly concerned with issues of 'recruitment and organisation'. The composite carried on 'recruitment' at the 36th BDC (1995) still envisaged that this work would be carried out primarily by existing full-time officers and lay activists, but it did call for 'appropriate funding to be provided to support and sustain this programme for growth'.[12]

By the time of the 37th BDC (1997), a composite motion very clearly highlighted this issue; some of the US and Australian themes were starting to emerge in the narrative as well. Replying to the debate, Margaret Prosser said:

> [R]ecent successes ... in Region 4 at Grundig where teams of young people, staff and officers, women and men had a successful recruitment campaign pairing *like with like* ... Welcoming the £2 million allocated to recruitment and organisation ... an action weekend to take place in November ... to share experiences and plan the way forward in plenary and workshop sessions. There would be guest speakers from the TUC, the United States and Australia who would also share their experiences with delegates.[13]

At the 38th BDC it was recognised that perhaps existing employees may not always be best placed to shoulder this new task of organising; Margaret Prosser again replying to the debate on 'Recruitment' said: 'the Executive had also agreed that Regions could take on dedicated recruiters working to the parameters set out in the Action Plan'.[14]

12 Minutes of the Proceedings of the 36th Biennial Delegate Conference 1995, p.41.
13 Minutes of the Proceedings of the 37th Biennial Delegate Conference 1997, pp.38–39. Emphasis added.
14 Minutes of the Proceedings of the 38th Biennial Delegate Conference 1999, p.19.

Organising Migrant Workers in the Hospitality Industry

Dave Turnbull (interview, 4 February 2021)

The hospitality industry presented very different challenges for organising agendas. Migrant workers have been seen as particularly difficult to organise. However, they have brought specific strengths too, as experiences in hospitality illustrate, with a history of trade union organising from the 1980s and even before that. From 1984 the Greater London Council (GLC) under Ken Livingstone's leadership had provided funding to support this organising work, via the Service Workers Action and Advisory Project, bringing leads from different unions together – T&G, GMB, USDAW (the Union of Shop, Distributive & Allied Workers) and the Tailors' and Garment Workers' Union – to organise service industry workers.

This had been the context in which Dave Turnbull (now a Unite Regional Officer with national responsibility for the hospitality industry) had become involved in organising work in the hospitality industry. Barry Camfield had been the Region 1 Education Officer at that time. He had been very clear about the interconnections between education and organising, seeing the common ground between them. Together they had organised a number of weekend sessions for the hospitality sector activists at the union's residential centre in Eastbourne, sessions in which organising had been a central theme. By the early 1990s Dave had trained as a tutor and then gone on to become a full–time official, gaining responsibility for the hospitality sector from 1992/1993.

This was a vulnerable sector. Two-tier workforces were increasingly common, with agency workers – including migrant agency workers – coming into the more vulnerable jobs. There were 'new ways of working' – old-fashioned forms of exploitation, in other words. But migrant workers had brought their own histories of militancy with them. Politically and industrially well-educated workers had arrived from parts of Latin America (including places with repressive regimes, such as Colombia) and from Spain and Portugal (places that had experienced repression under military governments), as well as from the Philippines and Cyprus. Many of these activists were refugees – and politically conscious already. (More recent migrants have tended to have different, and less directly political, backgrounds.)

Developing Organising Agendas in Hotel and Catering

Turnbull referred to the influence of Pete Hagger, who had, in response to the Thatcher government's onslaught on the trade union movement, clearly recognised the need for organising, speaking to the branches, developing strategies for organising the unorganised.

Another factor had been the establishment of the Advisory Committee for

Hotel and Catering within the Food, Drink & Tobacco Trade Group. This had facilitated the development of wider co-ordinated organising agendas, from the bottom up rather than from the top down. There had been previous attempts at a national organising campaign (for example, in relation to the Ladbroke Hilton chain.) But this had been a one-off, short-term initiative.

By the early 1990s it had become clear that it was going to be very difficult to run successful campaigns for recognition (although there *were* some successful campaigns for recognition subsequently, among Eurostar catering stewards and among some casinos). So, by the early 1990s, the focus was mostly on campaigning around particular issues and building up the membership in the branches.

The Employment Relations Act 1999 did make a difference subsequently (although this didn't enable a campaign for recognition at the Dorchester Hotel to succeed – this had to be withdrawn on a technicality). But the legislation was useful in general, even if its usefulness was limited. The right to be represented was actually more important in the hospitality industry. This legislation had been concentrated on individual grievances though – attempts to take collective grievances had not been allowable as it turned out, as the employers realised that they could insist that each case be taken separately.

There were continuing challenges, however. There were still some full-time officials who were not so involved – although many, probably most, were supportive. There were also questions about the extent to which there was a strategy for organising low-paid workers *per se*. This remains a challenge.

In Turnbull's view, there had also been a gap (an overlapping gap) in terms of a national strategy to organise those in precarious employment/organising the unorganised (which had been a key feature of earlier approaches within T&G). There was a period when there came to be more focus on recruitment numbers, increasing density in already partially organised contexts. Was this about going for the low-hanging fruit, avoiding risk-taking?

Organising workers in precarious employment was necessarily going to involve risks. And there seems to have been some reluctance to take on risky challenges. People wanted to be associated with success rather than with failure. But if there had been no risk taking there would not have been the 1889 Dock Strike, he pointed out!

Some regions and areas (for example, London and the South East, Northern Ireland and Scotland, Liverpool and Manchester) had recognised these arguments and focused on putting their energies into organising the unorganised – including low-paid and precarious workers in hospitality. But others had not. Unless workers in the hotel and catering sector had past industrial experience already, though, they were not going to organise by themselves. They did need support from officials.

Despite the problems, there were significant achievements from the 1990s into the twenty-first century. The impetus was from the bottom up, especially in

London, Glasgow and Belfast. Resources for organising in the hospitality sector had not been forthcoming from the top in the past although it had become easier to get back-up resources subsequently because of the wider recognition of the importance of the organising agenda.

Still, there were remaining gaps in terms of the organisation of precarious workers, leaving the way open for these gaps to be filled by newer, smaller non-TUC 'independent' unions. But these newer, smaller unions lacked the resources to provide adequate support for the longer term.

Tony Woodley, the Organising Department and Sharon Graham

This evolution of organising as a discrete theme or practice was very evident at the 39th BDC held in 2001, with conference carrying a comprehensive composite motion on 'Recruitment and Organisation'. The early years of the twenty-first century were marked by an intensification of this work, with the election of Tony Woodley as General Secretary in 2003, elected on a platform of massively increasing efforts and resources given over to organising.

Riding on the crest of a wave after the campaign to keep the Longbridge car plant open and winning the Deputy General Secretary election when Margaret Prosser retired, in his campaign to be T&G General Secretary Tony Woodley had decided that organising would be the 'big idea' that marked him out from the other candidates.

One of Woodley's key advisors, Len McCluskey, had suggested that there needed to be a new department established within the union, an Organising Department. Although concerned about the financial burden, Woodley, after he became General Secretary, agreed and the union nationally proceeded to appoint organisers, in the first period on fixed-term contracts. In this initial phase the new department came under Jack Dromey's area of responsibility; he had been elected Deputy General Secretary to fill the vacancy caused by Woodley's election as General Secretary. Sharon Graham was appointed second in command of the new department, and was designated Director of Organising in 2005.

Although Woodley was elected on an organising ticket, this would not mean signing up to the TUC Organising Academy. As Sharon Graham notes 'what was evident from our experience was that organisers being trained through the TUC Academy [of which she was one] had not been trained on the type of organising that the T&G wanted to adopt – therefore we knew we would have to grow our own'.[15] This was not at all surprising as the year prior to Woodley's election the TUC had launched the

15 S. Graham, 'Organising out of decline – the rebuilding of the UK and Ireland

Partnership Institute. If the Organising Academy was to engender workers' self-reliance to rebuild the movement from the bottom up, the promotion of partnership with (just a few as it turned out) employers reeked to many of class collaboration.

The TUC was trying to ride both horses at once; Woodley was hardly likely to go along with this approach as he was clearly a leading light of what was becoming known as the 'Awkward Squad' – a set of newly-elected general secretaries who were extremely dissatisfied with the TUC's New Realism, an accommodation with neo-liberalism, and Tony Blair's neo-liberal New Labour.

The T&G proceeded to develop its own unique approach to organising. This approach started with an explicit rejection of many of the failed initiatives of the recent past, for example the provision of added services to members – discounted insurance, holiday schemes and union-endorsed credit cards. Further, it rejected the idea of recruiting or organising employers to deliver a passive membership to the union, presumably through the signing of a 'partnership agreement'.

Although having the same starting point as the TUC, the workplace leader, the T&G sought to take this to a whole different plane with workplace leaders – shop stewards – active at workplace, industry and global levels. As explained by Sharon Graham:

> [T]he three elements of T&G Organising are built upon one central core – the need to develop effective workplace leaders. Without effective workplace organisation – the ability to act collectively to maximise bargaining power in order to defend and raise standards – then it is impossible to operate and rebuild successfully at either the national site, company and industry level or the global company and industry level. Without effective organising globally we cannot realistically expect to achieve long term sustainable success at home.[16]

In short, the TUC objective with the turn to organising could be said to be about increasing union *presence* at work, typified by the almost simultaneous launch of the Organising Academy and the Partnership Institute, whereas the T&G approach was concerned with increasing union *power* at work. For a more contemporary discussion of organising for union power readers should consult the most recent work by veteran US union organiser, Jane McAlevey.[17]

shop stewards movement' (2007) http://employees.org.uk/annual-report-TGW.html, p.4. Originally published by Union Ideas Network.

16 Graham, 'Organising out of decline', p.3.

17 J.F. McAlevey, *No Shortcuts: Organising for Power in The new Gilded Age* (OUP, 2016).

The T&G Organising Department was established in June 2005. In its first two years of operation, Sharon Graham notes that it had organised 15,000 new members to the union, concentrated in four industrial sectors:

- meat processing;
- low-cost airlines;
- building services (cleaning);
- logistics.[18]

Meat processing and contract cleaning were consolidated in the newly created head office Organising Department after initially being mainly Region 1 campaigns. Graham says:

> [I]n the meat sector we have not just increased industry membership and won recognition at all the major market players, we have implemented a growing sector-wide bargaining strategy. This has been achieved through the development of a 'meat combine' for shop stewards to drive issues on a sectoral basis – maximising bargaining power. Through this sector combine we have already used our client strategy to move on the issue of excessive agency working at sites and pay parity. For the first time the key processing companies and their supermarket customers are having to deal with such issues in the face of united industry wide trade union organisation – all shop stewards pushing for the same agenda building pressure through increased power.[19]

The union's success in contract cleaning is described by Sharon Graham: [T]he success of the client strategy in the London cleaning campaign has delivered another vital message – leverage is paramount. With the able assistance of Grant Williams of the SEIU we have now forced the vast majority of cleaning contractors in the City of London and Canary Wharf to sign 'zonal agreements' with the union. We have done this by putting at stake the reputation of key clients. Well-organised daily demonstrations against clients who would prefer to accept the possibility of paying a marginal increase in cost rather than have their reputation tarnished has proved hugely successful. The clients have used their clout with the contractors to force them to the table and sign agreements with the union. All agreements are zonal based agreements locking contractors into what in effect becomes one bargaining unit. This approach has been developed to increase the power of disparate cleaners, increase the likelihood of sustainable progress at the bargaining table and prevent the possibility of companies undercutting each other in a race to the bottom.[20]

18 Graham, 'Organising out of decline', p.5.
19 Graham, 'Organising out of decline', p.5.
20 Graham, 'Organising out of decline', p.5.

Organising in the White Meat Industry

Orlando Martins (interview, 4 February 2021)

Chris Kaufman, Tony Gould, Ivan Crane, Teresa Mackay

& Barry Salmon (roundtable, 10 February 2021)

The white meat sector was a prime target for organising. This was a labour-intensive industry. Bernard Matthews was a major focus because it was already organised, although membership density was not high. From 2000 onwards this was a strategic choice as a focus for organising. The aim was not just to recruit members but to organise them to enable them to fight on their own behalf. This was very different from simply focusing on recruitment.

There was to be an emphasis upon organising and enabling workers to take responsibility for taking up their own issues rather than just relying on officials, building on previous experiences of organising in the union. There had been gains in the past, in terms of increasing membership – especially when there was a dispute, and the union could negotiate a good settlement. But it was more of a struggle to get the membership active to do it for themselves.

Orlando Martins, who is Portuguese, emerged as an informal leader; his English was good, so he became recognised as a source of information, advice and support, resulting in him being elected as a shop steward. The achievement of real strength depended on encouraging the whole workforce to get involved and become active – and this still applies not only in the white meat industry but across the whole labour force in different industries.

But there was some reluctance within the union to promote this approach too, especially with migrant workers. And the established union structures had not been set up to organise in this sense. There were problems organising migrant workers speaking a variety of languages, for example (especially from 2008 or so onwards, with the arrival of migrants from the new EU Accession States in eastern Europe).

There were added problems because eastern European migrants had very different experiences of trade unionism, which they tended to see in a very negative light. This was very different from the experiences and attitudes of migrant workers from Portugal and Spain, or from Latin American countries such as Colombia, for example – workers who did bring positive previous experiences of trade unionism.

The employment of migrant workers had indeed been problematic in a number of ways (not just in terms of language). For example, there had been resistance from British workers, expressed during a meeting with shop stewards to identify their key issues. In addition to shared concerns about pay, the issue that really provoked discussion was British workers' anxiety that migrant labour would be used to undercut pay and conditions. Their initial suggestion was that the answer was to send them all migrant labour home. But when this was explored more fully with them, they could see that the answer was to organise migrant workers too, to win equal treatment for all workers – including temporary/contract workers.

Organising teams would consist of three or four organisers. Orlando himself worked with three or four such teams, giving support, including support in relation to language. He used to refer workers to the colleges where they could learn English. Through this, the union became closer to these migrant workers, gaining their trust. This was essential, building relationships with them through the learning agenda. It was also important that Orlando was seen as one of them – being a migrant worker himself.

The organisers began by identifying key leaders in each group, workers who others looked up to with respect. This was the basis for organising, building relationships with informal leaders as the way in.

This approach had parallels with the organising model that the T&G had already developed, adapted from the US model, taking account of the variations between these different contexts. Having said that though – about the differences – Orlando pointed out that the situation did not differ all that much. In the UK, for instance, there were employers who hired union busters, just as there were examples of this in the US (although this may have been more prevalent over there).

Given such difficulties, it was important to reach workers through their own communities if they could not be safely reached at work. This was especially relevant on greenfield sites where there was no recognition as yet, no shop stewards and no access to the workers. Organisers would meet with migrant workers through the places where they gathered in towns such as Ipswich, Great Yarmouth and Norwich (for example, Portuguese cafes and Polish churches). Through these contacts they began to identify leaders and then to map the workplaces through these leaders. And to find out where workers would meet – where they would hang out.

The organisers would encourage informal leaders to go on to become more involved as shop stewards, and safety reps, for example. As a result, a number of workers with migrant backgrounds did go on to become reps. This was about developing self-sustaining structures

In addition to organising the workers themselves, the union also approached the big supermarkets who were buying the produce. This was to try to persuade them to act with responsibility as ethical traders. This approach was quite effective. The major supermarkets had been worried about their reputations. They wanted to be seen to be squeaky clean by their customers. The appalling mistreatment of migrant workers had become a very live issue at this time, giving this a high public profile. (This was in the context too of establishing the Gangmasters' Licensing Authority (2005)– which had been the result of campaigning following the death of cockle pickers in Morecambe Bay. This tragedy had drawn public attention to the great exploitation of migrant workers more generally.) So, getting the big supermarkets on board had been a key step.

It was very difficult to reach 100 per cent membership, despite all these efforts at different levels on the ground, through the shop stewards' combine as well as via wider national campaigning. But significant gains were achieved.

Ironically, the move away from payroll deductions actually made it easier to organise among vulnerable workforces. The payroll deductions system had meant that employers could see exactly who was – or was not – a member. Taking dues from members' individual bank accounts meant that employers no longer knew this – thereby protecting very vulnerable workers from less favourable treatment or even harassment by their bosses. In addition, employers had less idea about the actual strength of the union's membership – a factor that could be used to the union's advantage. 'It's better that way!' It was possible to bluff employers about the strength of membership in their workplace. 'They don't know how many members there actually are!' And in addition, when workers changed jobs, they still remained signed-up union members – another advantage for the union.

In summary, then, organising in Bernard Matthews and elsewhere was really quite successful overall – and still is. There have been national implications here as a result, as well as more specific implications for the white meat industry in East Anglia.

Problems and Challenges and How These Have Been Tackled

There had always been cases of obstruction from employers, for a start. When dealing with large firms it was very useful to have international links to share information about such employers via the International Union of Foodworkers in Geneva; via the shop stewards' combine it was possible to mobilise across all the different plants from a particular company.

Although it was difficult to recruit members in many rural situations, once recruited members did become active. This applied to the level of activism among agricultural workers in many rural situations. These were moral issues with wider political significance. Everyone knew everyone else in small rural communities and so it was possible to get widespread community support if workers were being treated unfairly.

The diversity of languages among migrant workers had also been a problem, as has already been mentioned. Bernard Matthews had gone to Portugal to recruit migrant workers – involving one other language as a result. This had been problem enough to tackle. But the language problem was considerably compounded when workers began to be recruited from eastern Europe from 2007/2008 onwards, bringing even greater diversity of languages.

Overall Achievements

Despite all these difficulties, great strides were made in organising in the white meat industry. Perseverance and consistent efforts were essential, focusing on issues that came from – and directly involved – the workforce in question. It was also essential to provide training for shop stewards so that they could pick up on these issues and provide continuing support on a longer-term basis. Education was key to building up effective organisation in fact.

The lessons were about organising, not just recruitment. There was so much to do, particularly given the changing composition of the workforce. There was so much to learn from the past in relation to agricultural work. But there were also so many lessons for the future. Campaigning in the white meat industry was at the cutting edge – with the example of cyber campaigning for illustration – getting into Marks & Spencer's website and posting messages about conditions in the workforces producing the items that they were selling. There were new ways of working here that could be applied across other sectors, nationally.

Orlando also stressed the importance of persistence – it is all about persistence. You need to keep on at this. The key is to identify two or three local leaders. And then you need to identify the right issue – the issue that is at the forefront of the workers' concerns. Although this may be pay, this is not always the most immediate issue. It might be the canteen; it might be about transport. It's not always about pay, first and foremost. He gave an example where the trigger had been the employers' decision that the workforce should use whatever wellington boots were available, sharing boots from other shifts, rather than having their own personal pair of wellingtons for work. This was simply unacceptable to the workforce.

So, it is always about finding the right people as leaders and working with them. And finding the issues that are most important to the workers. Campaigns need to be dictated 'by *them* not by *us*'.

The white meat combine was the first national industry combine set up by the T&G since the 1970s. Its success in organising led to the establishment of a similar red meat combine, which when they amalgamated, as the meat combine, chalked up the recruitment of 20,000 new members in the mid-noughties. This enabled the union to establish a number of ground-breaking achievements, including the winning of equal rights for part-time and temporary workers, often agency workers, with permanent staff. Bernard Matthews was the first big employer to sign up to the agreement, closely followed by the other major meat employers. It meant, for example, that agency workers would be taken on as permanent workers after 13 weeks.

Organising in the Contract Cleaning Sector

Miles Hubbard (interview, 21 January 2021)

Having graduated from the TUC Organising Academy and gained some experience in other unions, Miles Hubbard (now a Unite Regional Officer in East Anglia) had responded to an advertisement in *Tribune* to apply for a post with T&G Region 1, as an organiser.

Tony Woodley had been playing a key role here in his view, moving the union's approach forward at this time, developing a more strategic approach nationally, drawing on lessons from the US and elsewhere. This was the background for Miles Hubbard's involvement in the Canary Wharf campaign.

The campaign itself focussed on Morgan Stanley, Lehman Brothers, Credit Suisse and Bank of America. Each had their own contracts with major cleaning contractors, such as Mitie, ISS, Initial and others. The cleaning companies attempted to pass off responsibility onto the big banks, and the big banks attempted to pass off responsibility onto the contractors, each saying that the other was responsible. The campaign did not accept this – and it did succeed in making big waves, including in the press. But this was too much for one person to manage. Miles asked for more resources and was eventually given one other organiser, Rhys McCarthy.

As the campaign grew (by 2004) it developed momentum with a plan for a big demonstration 'Walk on the Wharf'. This planned demonstration was supported by different political groups on the left, with mobilisations being promoted everywhere, including plans to be promoted at the European Social Forum, a huge international anti-globalisation event that was being organised at Alexandra Palace at that time.

The employers responded with an injunction to stop the action. Ken Livingstone, as Mayor of London, had offered support to the demonstration, offering that the organisers could stand on TfL property at the tube station rather than on Canary Wharf itself. General Secretary Tony Woodley was in China and uncontactable at this time; Deputy General Secretary Jack Dromey did not feel in a position to risk court action – with the risks of associated costs. The organisers had to stand down, giving out repudiation notices at Alexandra Palace – in the face of taunts from the far left.

Miles believes that good activists came to the union from the Canary Wharf cleaners' campaign: Emmanuel Sillah, who is now working in the Unite Organising & Leverage Department and Jose Vallejo Villa, who turned up at the T&G office as a leader of the Latin American Workers' Association and is now a Regional Co-ordinating Officer in the London & Eastern Region of Unite.

The story illustrates the potential tensions between organising agendas and trade union structures, if and for whatever reason these structures are unable to provide the necessary backup support. The campaign had made an impact. But there were difficulties in following this through successfully, as a result leaving the terrain to smaller, community-based initiatives – with their own inherent limitations.

Reflections on Lessons for the Future

As those with experience of organising have reflected, T&G's experiences of organising show that there was no single model of organising that could be universally applied, but there were still important lessons to be drawn.

It was essential to start from workers' own priorities in terms of the issues. Officials typically start from pay – which is, of course, a key issue. But so are other issues such as bullying and fear; people feeling that they are being 'treated like slaves'. Pay was the strapline at Canary Wharf for instance, but bullying was also a key issue for the workers there. Unreasonable and unsafe working practices emerged as key issues elsewhere too, from the docks to the white meat industry.

Organising needed to start from the principle that 'like recruits like' identifying organic leaders *not* just mobilising experienced leaders, a principle that the TUC Organising Academy also recognised. But it was important not to expect too much of activists either. Activists need backup from officials working with them collaboratively. This finding emerged from T&G experiences across the sectors, as has already been discussed.

There needed to be sufficient resources for organising too – including, for example, organisers who could speak different languages. This had emerged as a factor across sectors, including, for instance, the white meat industry. And there needed to be recognition of the fact that organising is a highly skilled job. This had not necessarily been recognised within trade union structures initially, with younger and less senior staff working as organisers. It had been very challenging for these organisers to promote wider changes from such junior positions. The research study that followed up TUC Organising Academy graduates had come to similar conclusions, recommending that organising needed to be more fully integrated with wider strategies for change.[21]

It was also important to focus on workers in their communities, the *whole* worker – making the links between the workplace and the community – contacting workers outside the workplace and in the community where necessary, not exposing them to the risks of reprisals from rogue employers. This was a finding that had emerged from experiences within the T&G

21 Simms, Holgate & Heery, *Union Voices*.

from way back, as Jack Jones and others had found. The importance of making these links had continuing contemporary relevance, from the docks and cleaning sectors through to the white meat industry and elsewhere.

And it was essential to focus on the entire workforce inclusively – skilled, semi-skilled and unskilled workers, women as well as men, including part-time women workers and workers from BAEM communities in the service sector, identifying growth areas of employment, not just focusing on traditionally well-organised sectors. Organising was about building confidence and strength, moving from small gains onwards as part of longer-term strategies for empowerment, not just focusing on recruitment numbers or going for demobilising partnership deals.

As the T&G became Unite, the new union seemed uniquely well placed to build upon these experiences, drawing on its heritage, developing strategic approaches towards organising for the future. However, the road ahead and the transition to become an organising union would remain difficult, if not elusive. As one academic, very much sympathetic to the organising model, noted:

> [T]he central organising department – large though it is – remains a bolt-on that hasn't been able to realise the stated aspiration to change overall culture of the union from that of servicing to organising. In practice, ... since adopting its 'strategy for growth', the full- time officers have little to do with the activities of the organising department (and vice versa), and this division is not conducive to building the strategic capacity needed for effective change and transformation of the union.[22]

22 J. Holgate, *Arise: Power, Strategy and Union Resurgence* (Pluto Press, 2021), p.179.

4

The T&G and the Equality Agenda

Mary Davis

There can be no doubt that the pinnacle of the long campaign to win meaningful progress for women members of the T&G was reached when a major rule change was passed in 1998. The new rules implemented the principle of 'minimum proportionality'. Once established, it was impossible to deny this same principle of representation to Black members of the union. In this respect women can rightly be credited with paving the way for other under-represented groups in the long battle for equality. But although the rule change applied to Black groups too, it was not implemented immediately.

Recounting the steps by which these historic changes were made in one of the largest UK trade unions is a case study in the principle of self-organisation combined with steadfast campaigning in challenging the historic pale and male image of the trade union movement.[1] This chapter will focus on how this important transformation was accomplished.

The achievement of this change was the culmination of many years of constant campaigning by women in the union, led by the first self-organised group in the T&G: the National Women's Advisory Committee (NWAC), chaired by Jane McKay, together with its regional counterparts (RWACs). Recounting the steps by which the rule change on women's representation was achieved not only throws light on the long battle for equal representation, but also on the strategy and tactics to achieve it. It is abundantly clear that self-organisation was the key to success.

Women

In practice, for women, the rule change meant that 'as a minimum every T&G constitutional committee and conference had to include the

---

1 Self-organisation is not a term used by the T&G; its preference is to use 'structures to ensure women's (or Black) voice in the union'. However, I have used 'self-organisation' throughout as a more commonly used and less cumbersome term.

proportion of women it represents'.[2] This included every regional and national trade group, district, regional and national committees and all delegate conferences. However, an exception to the proportionality rule was implemented for the GEC because, as the amendment passed at the Rules Conference stated, its composition 'is subject to statute' and would thus 'require additional reserved seats'.[3]

Volume 5 of this work has traced both the consistent campaign and the disappointingly slow progress of women's equality in the TGWU during the 1980s. In recognition of the snail-paced change, the 1993 BDC set targets for women's representation. However, despite good intentions, it was recognised three years later in 1996 that the 'T&G 1993 BDC policy has led to the achievement of very limited progress in the representation of T&G women members'.[4] The debate at the GEC in June 1996 went further – it was critically forthright in its assessment of the lack of progress. It acknowledged the following:

- For the overwhelming majority of constitutional committees, the 1993 BDC policy had led to no progress and, in some areas, to a decline in women's representation.

- Based on progress to date, although targets might be reached in a few specific areas, there was no prospect of achieving proportional representation of T&G women throughout the union by 1998, in line with BDC policy.

- Women's under-representation within the union had not been successfully tackled in practice by the 1993 BDC policy.

In view of this highly critical acknowledgment of failure to implement conference policy on women's representation, the GEC agreed, somewhat tamely, to 'monitor this matter and to report to council in due course'.[5] Such timidity was based on the GEC's observation that 'changing the culture of the union takes time' and that dealing with 'women's involvement' was not easy or 'likely to bear fruit overnight'.[6] Clearly, merely setting targets had not worked.

Two years later, in 1998 a special GEC received a comprehensive report reviewing women's representation in the union.[7] It was wide ranging, covering both the work of the NWAC in furthering policies for women in the workplace and in the union. In respect of the former, it was clear

---

2 1999 National Women's Committee Guidance, 'Encouraging women's participation in T&G', Diana Holland (DH) archive.
3 GEC amendment agreed at 1998 Rules Conference.
4 GEC, June 1996, Minute no.353.
5 GEC, June 1996, Minute no.353.
6 GEC, June 1996, Minute no.734.
7 *Representation of Women in the T&G*, April 1998, DH archive.

that the union, guided by its Equality Strategy 1995–2000 and the 1997 BDC policy on women's recruitment, had made considerable progress in formulating negotiating strategies on such issues as sexual harassment, domestic violence, maternity leave and reproductive health and safety.

However, this was not matched by progress on women's representation within the T&G. This was despite the fact that although male membership of the union had fallen by 10,000 in the period 1996–1997, women's membership had increased by 2,000 and thus, the report argued, the BDC motion[8] on 'Organisation' was of vital importance. This motion stated that women's recruitment was a 'top priority' for the union, but that this could only be achieved if the T&G could demonstrate to women that 'we understand and prioritise their key concerns'.[9] Noting the failure of the 1993 policy of target setting, the report acknowledged that, although further efforts had been made to increase women's representation in proportion to their numbers, the outcome of the 1997 election to the various union committees was disappointing. None of the T&G's eight regional committees had achieved their target for proportional representation. Only five of the 14 national trade group committees had done so. The GEC, however, was the only committee to achieve its target – it now contained six women, representing 19 per cent of the total female membership.[10] The conclusion was obvious: the figures clearly showed that 'the BDC Policy alone has not successfully tackled the under-representation of women in our union'.[11]

It was by now abundantly clear to the NWAC that a new initiative was needed. The voluntary method had failed and compulsion via a rule change was the only answer. Thus, the report concluded that 'effective and fair representation of women and men in the T&G can only be guaranteed through enshrining this policy in the T&G Rule Book'.[12] The report recommended that a new clause be inserted in Rule 3 (Constitution and Government) that would require 'all committees and conferences of the union to ensure at least proportionate representation of women', and that this would also mean consequential amendments on rules governing each and every conference and committee. In addition the NWAC was concerned to ensure that women's committees at regional and national level 'have statutory status in rule with the right to have full voting and representation rights on Regional Committees and a national women's seat on the General Executive Council'[13] and, in common with trade

8 Composite Motion 52 on organisation.

9 Composite Motion 52 on organisation.

10 However, as the report noted, this was '1% less than the growing % of women in the union because of rounding down'.

11 *op cit* p.2.

12 *ibid* p.7.

13 *ibid* p.8.

group representatives, this seat would be elected by the constituency it represented – in this case by women only. With such deft moves, the women of the T&G devised an impregnable strategy to ensure a fulsome recognition of their rights and representation. In July 1998 the Rules Conference agreed to these changes: but in addition it also reaffirmed that the same principle of proportionality be applied to BAME members and that this should be implemented no later than 2003. Jane McKay, who moved the successful Rule amendments which were agreed with no votes against made the powerful argument 'women needs unions, yes, but unions need women'.

Bill Morris, the T&G General Secretary at the time, was, in the words of Margaret Prosser, 'always supportive of the equalities agenda'.[14] He backed the rule change, but argued that, although it represented a major step forward, 'it cannot be the end of the story. Now the structures are in place, we need to develop the culture to match. Proportionality, while important, represents just one step towards true equality. It is a means and not the purpose itself'.[15]

When Margaret Prosser retired as Deputy General Secretary of the T&G in 2002 (having served as Women's Officer from 1985 to 1998), she was interviewed in the T&G magazine for women members in which she was described as 'one of the highest profile women in the trade union and labour movement'. When asked what she regarded as her proudest achievement in the T&G, she replied: 'I'm proudest of starting the debate that led to the introduction of proportionality. When I began we still had to convince people about the need for positive action to get women involved'. However when asked if there was anything she regretted, her answer confirmed Bill Morris' view that proportionality on its own was not enough: 'though we've gone a long way in encouraging women, younger people and black people to take part in the union, the T&G is still very male and very white. It's likely that both Bill [Morris] and I will be succeeded by white men, and when I go there will only be one executive officer'.[16]

Prosser's fears proved to be correct. The lone executive officer remaining was Diana Holland, (a long-standing champion of women's rights) who had succeeded Margaret Prosser as National Women's Officer, later National Secretary for Women. In 2006 Diana was promoted to Assistant General Secretary with the much expanded brief of Women, Race and Equalities – a post that she held until her retirement in the merged union, Unite.

Following the rule change, detailed guidance on its implementation was issued, which took into account the fact that 'electoral procedures

---

14 Interview with M. Prosser, *Together*, issue 28, Summer 2002.
15 *Together*, issue 20, Winter 2000.
16 *Together*, issue 20, Winter 2000.

and committee structures in the T&G vary in each region'.[17] However, such implementation was to be based on the principle adopted by the Rules Conference, which was 'not to increase overall representation but to ensure that it is proportionate'.[18] But it was recognised that some flexibility must be exercised where the constituency concerned had a small number of women and where the seat allocation was also small. In such cases minimum proportionality might be unachievable, and so additional seats for women should be proposed.

Welcome as the rule change was, it was recognised that, on its own, it would not address the many years in which women members had been marginalised. Tackling their under-representation would only be successful if the union took meaningful steps to encourage women's greater involvement in the affairs of the union. Proportionality was not enough, As Prosser and Morris had said, it was the beginning, and not the end, of the journey to changing the culture of the union. The 1989 BDC recognised that women's working lives must be part of all decision-making, and hence it was necessary to take positive steps at all levels to redress the under-representation of women within the union as workplace representatives, on workplace committees, branch committees and as Regional Industrial Organisers. The motion went on to detail the necessary step to achieve this:

- improving the involvement and participation of women members in the workplace, branch, district, trade groups, regional and national activities, including the creation of posts for branch women's equality officers and women's representatives at the workplace;

- ensuring that women are properly represented in lay member non-constitutional industrial committees and conferences at all levels;

- continuing to encourage women's participation in T&G education and equal opportunities education for all T&G members;

- women's participation to be encouraging all women – BAEM women, young women and disabled women;

- developing positive action programmes to encourage women members to become Regional Industrial Organisers;

- ensuring that the T&G equal opportunities policy is fully and actively implemented.[19]

17 *Consultation Paper on Proportionate Representation of Women* (GEC, December 1998), DH archive.
18 GEC September 1998, Minute 521.
19 1989 BDC Minutes.

The first election in 2000 under the new rule on women's representa-tion did not fully result in minimum proportionality. Seven out of eight regional committees met the rule requirement and 11 out of 14 trade groups similarly. However, this is partly explained by the fact that two trade groups, Docks and Waterways and Building Construction and Civil Engineering, had insufficient women members to enforce the rule.

Black Members

Although the guidance issued in 1998 on the implementation of the rule change was primarily concerned with securing proportionality for women members, the rule change had also applied to Black members – now referred to as Black and Asian ethnic minority members, which the T&G said was in accordance with the then current equal opportunities monitoring definitions. The rule change stated: 'From no later than the Rules Conference to be held in 2004 Black and Asian ethnic minority representation of elected delegates shall be proportionate to the respective membership of the Region'.

However, implementing this rule change for Black members was not possible without knowledge of the numerical composition of this section of the union's membership – a task that could only be accomplished by ethnic monitoring. Thus it was recognised that fulfilling the rule change would be delayed until monitoring was completed. Making headway on this was slow. A motion carried at the 1989 BDC stated that, despite the national committees being given data on the ethnic identification of members in their trade group, along with an action plan, including survey material, very little progress had been made. Awareness of racism and the need to empower Black members within the union structures was clearly still a matter to be addressed. The BDC motion thus called for:

> The administration to provide full information on ethnic monitoring each quarter of all newly joined members and to ensure that strong measures are taken to record the ethnicity of all other members who are registered as 'unidentified'.
>
> Conference therefore calls upon the GEC to actively promote the completion and return of monitoring forms. There should also be a campaign to raise the awareness and understanding amongst our members of the importance of monitoring. Recognising that one of the key areas for this campaign should be through the Union's education structure.[20]

20 1999 BDC Minutes: Motion on Ethnic Monitoring.

Part of the rule change for BAEM members had been implemented in 1999. National and regional Race Equality Committees had been established as full T&G constitutional committees. Also a national BAEM representative had been elected to serve on the GEC. This was part one of a two-stage process – minimum proportionality was the next stage. As with women, detailed guidance was issued in 2003 on the implementation of the rule change on T&G committees.[21] This guidance was similar to that issued for women's minimum proportionality in 1998 and attempted to circumvent the problems encountered then.

The BDC 2001 recognised that there was still much to be done in relation to ethnic monitoring. But this was not the only concern. A motion from the National Women's Committee and the National Race Equality Committee (Composite 8), welcomed the rule change, but stated that: 'For proportional representation to have a real effect on equality in our Union, we must ensure that Black, Asian and ethnic minority members are encouraged and supported in playing a full role. Union education courses to address this are very important'. It went on to call for the GEC to reinforce the union's commitment to addressing under-representation of BAEM members and to ensure their inclusivity.

Women, Race and Equalities

In 2000 the T&G created a new sector – Women, Race and Equalities (WR&E) – with Diana Holland as the National Organiser for WR&E, Colette Cork-Hurst as National Secretary for Equalities and Sharon Graham as National Secretary for Youth and Development. The status of WR&E was equivalent to that of the union's industrial sectors and hence this move signalled a much greater degree to which the equality agenda was embedded in the work of the union. The rationale for the creation of the WR&E was inspired by the new EU framework directives on race, sexual orientation and disability, all of which required amendments to existing UK law and which the Labour government proceeded to address.

Within the union's new WR&E sector the women's and race committees still organised at regional and local levels and had their own conferences and education programmes. However, this was supplemented in due course by addressing other equality issues, notably for and by disabled members, young members and LGBT (lesbian, gay, bisexual and transgender) members. The latter three established their own committees (beginning with a forum in the case of young members and a working

---

21 *Implementation of Race Equality Rules Agreed At 1998 Rules Conference on Regional & National Committees, Regional Trade Group/Sector & District Committees* (2003), DH archive.

party in the case of LGBT members) but, unlike race and women, these committees remained advisory only. One of the dangers in establishing an over-arching sector was that the concerns of individual equality groups would be blurred in an amorphous equality miasma. This was not to be the case in the T&G. Both the race and women's committees took steps to retain their own hard-fought right to self-organisation.

The BDC of 2001 welcomed the establishment of the new sector, but sought to ensure that the continuing positive role of the T&G Women's Conference[22] was maintained. The motion argued: 'Women remain under-represented in membership of our great union and the Women's Conference plays a vital role in organising women across the union, the wider labour movement and beyond'.[23]

Unlike many other unions which later merged their equality structures, the T&G continued to both recognise and support separate equality demographics, but at the same time sought to ensure that were common threads rather than competition between them. Thus periodic meetings were held between the chairs and vice-chairs of the five committees within the WR&E sector, the first meeting of which was held in 2003. Chaired by Jane McKay, the meeting agreed to draw up a joint action plan for the entire equalities sector, the detail to be discussed by the five constituent committees. The result of this would be drawn together and, in particular, 'areas of joint working and overlap'[24] would be identified. This resulted in an eight-page *Strategic Action Plan*, which was presented for endorsement to the 2003 BDC. This meeting also established an important principle that minimum proportionality 'must be minimum and not become the maximum'.[25]

The *Strategic Action Plan* detailed plans for each of the discrete sectors as well as overall priorities for all of them collectively. These included prioritising education on equality issues, tackling under-representation and ensuring that WR&E concerns featured in collective bargaining agendas.

2003–2009: New General Secretary, Unite and the T&G Section – the Impact on Equalities

In 2003 Tony Woodley replaced Bill Morris as T&G General Secretary. Four years later, in 2007, the T&G merged with Amicus to form Unite. Both unions became sections of Unite and their respective General Secretaries (Derek Simpson for Amicus, Tony Woodley for the T&G) remained in post as Joint General Secretaries. The Executive Councils of

22 To date, three T&G women's conferences had been held: 1995 'It's Time for Women', 1998 'Making a Difference for Women' and 2000 'New Beginnings'.
23 2001 BDC Minutes, Motion 50.
24 WR&E Meeting of Chairs & Vice-Chairs, August 2003, DH archive.
25 WR&E Meeting of Chairs & Vice-Chairs, August 2003, DH archive .

the predecessor unions became a Joint Executive Council, which served until elections could be held for an Executive Council of Unite. The new council took office on 1 May 2008. In July 2008, following a postal ballot of members, a new rule book for the new union was put in place.

Bill Morris was widely regarded as having championed the equality agenda in the T&G – Woodley was anxious to show that he was similarly supportive. At his first meeting of the GEC as General Secretary in December 2003, Woodley reported that the union had published a new guide to achieving race equality at work. It was needed, he said, because 'over a quarter of a century after race discrimination in employment was made unlawful, the union continues to see an increase in cases and is taking action to ensure that negotiators in all sectors are able to effect positive change to race relations in their workplace'.[26] He noted the that the Race Relations (Amendment) Act 2000 had widened the opportunities to protect public sector members and to actively promote race equality, but he urged that 'all our members, representatives and officers must be part of making all race law a reality'.

The Labour government had announced in its election manifesto of 2005 that it intended to introduce a Single Equality Act.[27] The T&G had long championed this initiative. At the 2005 BDC, a motion[28] from the WR&E reiterated its concern that 'current equality laws are not as comprehensive as we would want, and looks to the proposed Single Equality Act and new Public Sector Equality Duties as an opportunity to strengthen these rights, to make them more accessible, and ensure wide-ranging support across the Union'. The motion also called for 'Equal Opportunities to be fully addressed in education and training for T&G Organisers, Shop Stewards and all National, Regional T&G Officers with the active involvement of the Women, Race & Equalities sector'.

For those women and Black members who had championed the equality agenda in the T&G for three decades, the question inevitably arose as to whether the gains they had made would be retained and extended in the new union. Tony Woodley addressed this concern in a special BDC in 2006, which was called in order to report on the merger talks with Amicus. In his keynote address he announced that the new union would be a 'union for equality' and that it would preserve 'everything T&G women, T&G black members have established down the years in our union'. This would mean maintaining national and regional conferences *and* committees for Women, Black members, disabled members, gay and lesbian members

---

26 General Secretary's Report, GEC Minute no.600, December 2003.

27 This became law in 2010 – it was the last piece of legislation by the Labour government before its election defeat that year. As a precursor to the Single Equality Act, the Labour government in 2007 merged the six equality 'strands' into a single Equality and Human Rights Commission (EHRC).

28 BDC 2005 Composite Motion 11, Minute no.40 – Bargaining for Equality.

and guaranteeing proportionality for women and black members on *every* constitutional committee and conference.[29] He ended by asking: 'Will the New Union need to do more? Yes, of course. No-one can say the fight for equality has been won – neither in the workplace nor in our own organisations. But now every group suffering discrimination and disadvantage will have a powerful constitutional platform to advance their case'.

All this was reinforced by the 2007 BDC which noted that: 'women are more likely to join trade unions than men and that black women are more likely to join than white women, women's representation becomes even more important today than ever before. Conference therefore calls on the T&G to promote and safeguard advances achieved'.[30] As if to prove the point, the final meeting of the National Women's Committee of Unite T&G section recorded the contribution that the T&G had made to advances for women and equalities, and that these achievements 'form strong foundations on which our new union Unite the Union, can build'.[31] The final meeting went on to report on the implementation of Rule 11 on equalities. While there was a commitment to ensuring that this, the proportionality rule, would be enshrined in the new union, 'urgent action' was still needed and it was clear that 'the procedures would not be perfect first time'. However, it was reported that it was agreed that the first Unite National Women's Committee would consist of 34 seats with a minimum of three seats from each region and at least proportional representation of Black women.

At the final meeting of the T&G's GEC, the General Secretary advised the council that he had reviewed the Executive Officer structure of the union in order to consider the impact the merger would have on the need to increase the involvement of women in the senior management team.[32] He thus wanted to ensure that two Assistant General Secretaries be appointed and that one of them would be responsible for equalities. The GEC supported this and pledged its determination to ensure that 'the equalities and diversity agendas will be at the heart of the new union carrying forward our progressive tradition. Unite must ensure equality for all its members and is fully reflective of the full diversity of the working class of Britain and Ireland'.[33]

29 The capital letters are Tony Woodley's.

30 BDC 2007 Minutes, Motion 44.

31 Diana Holland's speech, Minutes of the National Women's Committee of UNITE T&G section, 22 April 2009, DH archive.

32 GEC Minute no.7.6 – Appointment of Assistant General Secretaries.

33 GEC Minute no.7.6 – Appointment of Assistant General Secretaries .

The T&G and Other Unions

To a greater or lesser extent, all unions and the TUC addressed the equality agenda in this period. Although this chapter has concentrated solely on the T&G, its journey has to be seen in the context of the wider battle against racism and sexism in the labour movement. This was and remains both an ideological battle and a struggle for the meaningful inclusion of those the movement has ignored for most of its history – women and Black people.

Having charted the T&G's journey along the equality and inclusion road, how does it measure up against the record of other unions during this period? Was it in the vanguard or the guard's van – or somewhere in between? The South East Region of the TUC (SERTUC) conducted a periodic survey of equality in trade unions, the eighth of which, entitled *Treading Water*, was published in 2008. Although it was not intended as a comparative exercise, we can, nevertheless, draw some qualified conclusions from it, but only if we look at unions of a similar size and similar percentages of Black and women members.

Thus, although UNISON is of a roughly similar size to the T&G, it is a public sector union, and its women membership was much larger – 74 per cent (in 2008). In 2008 the T&G's only suitable and useful comparator in terms of its record on equalities was Amicus. Like the T&G, Amicus organised predominantly in the private sector. Although somewhat larger in membership terms (1.1 million) than the T&G (747,600), it had a similar percentage of women members – 27 per cent (26 per cent T&G). However, it had no record of the number of its BAME[34] members – the T&G figure was 9.4 per cent. (The T&G was one of the very few unions that had conducted ethnic monitoring.) Clearly Amicus did not have anything like a minimum proportionality rule or reserved seats, since it did not record the number of women or Black members on its executive committee. On all other indices of structural and policy gains for women and Black members, the T&G was ahead of many unions, including Amicus.

In addition to minimum proportionality for women and Black members, the T&G, by the time of the merger, had both a number of regional women's organisers and a national organiser for women, race and equalities, who were women's equality officers. Regional women's committees with representatives from industrial sector/districts nominated from branches elected by the membership were well established by the time of merger. This was also the case for BAEM members. The National Women's Committee and the National Race Equality Committee (NREC) elected by the regional women's committees and regional RECs were no longer advisory – they were established constitutional committees.

34 The term used by SERTUC.

The T&G produced the *Together* magazine for women members twice a year. The union had embarked on many initiatives to promote and develop women's involvement in the union, in addition to rule book minimum proportionality: more women reps/union equality reps in male-dominated industries; ensuring that the development of the union equality rep role was complementary and not an alternative women's and race reps; ensuring women and other under-represented members were supported to become shop stewards; and promoting branch guidance on building women's involvement. In terms of initiatives to promote women's equality, the T&G had compiled information on women in the workforce to strategically target women's organisation and representation; used new family friendly rights, zero tolerance and equal pay campaigns to promote the union with women workers and as part of organising strategies. The union held regional and national women's courses, including an annual women's school of four separate courses with joint plenary sessions of all. There was much else besides.

Similar structural and policy changes were also in place for BAME members, which had a national secretary for equalities and designated regional race equality officers. Regional Race Equality Committees (RREC) with representatives from industrial sectors/districts nominated from branches, districts and trade groups and elected by the membership were in place. The T&G ran campaigns in workplaces with high numbers of BAEM workers encouraging them to become involved with recruitment and organisation. This included producing application forms and recruitment materials available online in 27 different languages. It produced information on organisation and recruitment of BAEM workers and produced a DVD *Hear Our Story – BAEM members speak out*.

Although comparisons are odious, it was clear that although, in common with all unions, Amicus had pursued an equality agenda, its structures and policies for rectifying the historic exclusion of women and Black members were not as advanced or embedded as those of the T&G. This explains the insistence of the latter to ensure that the T&G's long fought for equality gains were embedded in the new merged union – Unite. The T&G was successful – the resolution of its final BDC before merger paid tribute to all those 'T&G members and officials who have been working and campaigning tirelessly to achieve equality for women in the union, the workplace and in society. Conference notes that T&G has made great strides in its struggle for women's representation and equality as a whole and as ever we will only move forwards and never backwards'.[35]

---

35 BDC 2007 Minute – Women, Race and Equalities.

5

Politics – Home and Away

The period of the 'New' Labour government under Tony Blair and Gordon Brown from 1997 to 2010 is, of course, about two-thirds of the time span allocated to this volume. Taken from the point at which Blair became party leader in 1994, this makes 'New' Labour the most significant actor on the political stage. This chapter is most wide ranging in examining the union's relationship with the Labour Party, where it made no progress, and where it had some success. Initially, we examine Tony Blair's breakthrough as leader of the Labour Party, most definitely part of the trend identified by Stuart Hall, just prior to Margaret Thatcher becoming Prime Minister, as the 'Great Moving Right Show'.[1] Part of this tacking to the right would involve constantly seeking ways to diminish the union role in the party, particularly in the selection of the leader and parliamentary candidates and, at it apex, breaking the link between the affiliated unions and the party altogether.

We examine the divergent development of policy on trade union rights; the Labour leadership was most insistent that there would be no repeal of the Thatcher era anti-union laws while, at the same time, the T&G was doggedly sticking with calls not just for repeal but for the development of a new framework of rights at work.

Devolution for Scotland, Wales and London was said to be something that Blair was not really interested in, but the union in all locations was certainly committed and we examine how that unfolded. Of course for Northern Ireland Blair was intensely interested, as the restoration of devolved government in the North was an integral part of the peace process and his legacy. As far as London was concerned, Blair most definitely did not want Ken Livingstone as the Labour candidate for Mayor; Livingstone was someone who the T&G had worked closely with in the GLC days and was very likely to support.

---

1 S. Hall, 'The Great Moving Right Show', *Marxism Today*, January 1979.

Finally, we examine some international issues where the union had only a slight influence on Blair's foreign policy, committed as he was to wars of liberal intervention and moving in lock step with US foreign policy.

Tony Blair's Accession to the Labour Leadership

In 1992, after leading Labour to two general election defeats – in one he was said to have snatched defeat from the jaws of victory – Neil Kinnock resigned as leader of the Labour Party. Kinnock's own political journey had moved from the soft left Tribunite wing of the party to what became known as the 'modernisers' – essentially on the right of the party, but with a shiny new image that would be taken to new heights by Tony Blair.

An electoral college arrangement for the election of party leader and deputy leader had been instituted in 1981, with the affiliated unions holding 40 per cent of the votes, the Parliamentary Labour Party (PLP) 30 per cent and the Constituency Labour Parties (CLP) 30 per cent. CLPs were obliged to hold a 'one member, one vote' (OMOV) ballot to determine their preference on a 'winner takes all' basis.

Kinnock may have lost the 1987 general election, but in defeat there was at least one winner. The party's communications manager, Peter Mandelson, started to exert his malign influence over the party. It was from this point forward that the seismic shift in relations between the party and the affiliated unions became apparent, as noted by Andrew Murray: 'it was after 1987 that the "modernising" project really got under way in the Labour Party with the unions, for the first time, being seen as an embarrassing liability'.[2]

Kinnock was succeeded as leader by John Smith. At the same time, the party's National Executive Committee resolved to establish a Trade Union Review Group, which would examine the trade union–party link, particularly in connection with the election of leader and deputy leader and in the selection of parliamentary candidates. Smith had made it clear that his own preference was for reform in these areas. Reform was invariably code for a diminished role for the unions.

According to academic Wickham-Jones:

Smith's preference was for two fundamental reforms to the party's constitution. The electoral college would be redefined with equal shares given to MPs and members thus excluding the trade unions from participation in it. Candidate selection would take place on the basis of OMOV. Implacably opposed to such proposal, the

---

2 Murray, *New Labour Nightmare*, p.31.

vast majority of Labour's affiliated unions mobilized considerable support against them.[3]

In the period leading to the 1993 party conference there was agreement that OMOV would be extended to the unions in voting for leader and deputy leader; the union votes would be allocated to candidates in proportion to votes cast, and the union share of the electoral college would reduce from 40 per cent to one-third.

There was no agreement on removing the unions from parliamentary selections. However, a last-minute decision to abstain by the Manufacturing, Science & Finance Union (MSF) allowed the Smith view to prevail.

Also in 1993, apparently acting on the advice of former President of the National Union of Journalists (NUJ) Dennis McShane, Bill Morris put on a prestigious seminar entitled 'Clintonomics', with a clutch of Clinton advisors including Elaine Kamarck, Paul Begala and Stan Greenberg:

> Morris agreed that the T&G would put forward £50,000 to sponsor a landmark event to debate 'Clintonomics' at London's QE2 conference centre. [Margaret] Prosser recalls that Morris was certainly excited by Clinton's victory ... MacShane meanwhile saw Gordon and Tony walking from breakout session to breakout session absolutely gawping in awe at the wave of Americans, of their own generation, exuding success, achievement and confidence.[4]

There was a free flow of ideas across the Atlantic between the Democrats around Clinton and the Blair/Brown group in the Labour Party The unspoken rationale for the seminar was presumably to put Morris onside politically and ideologically with the new Labour leadership team and also to soften up the union for acceptance of what we now call globalisation, the essential message of the centrist Clinton project.

Totally unexpectedly, Smith died in May 1994, necessitating a new leadership election. Although no longer able to cast their votes as a block, unions had retained the right to nominate in the leader and deputy leader elections, but only seven of the 29 affiliated unions chose to do so in 1994. The T&G nominated Margaret Beckett, then seen to be on the left, or certainly to the left of Tony Blair.

Although perhaps not realised at the time, nomination of a candidate could well help in mobilising support. Nomination conferred an assumed

3 M. Wickham-Jones, 'Introducing OMOV: the Labour Party–Trade Union Review Group and the 1994 leadership contest', *British Journal of Industrial Relations*, 2014, vol.52, no.1, p.39.

4 R. Carr, *March of the Moderates: Bill Clinton, Tony Blair and the Rebirth of Progressive Politics* (IB Tauris, 2019), pp.179–180.

right for a nominating union to campaign among its members as, in 1994, the T&G did with strong support for Margaret Beckett from Bill Morris expressed in the pages of the union's journal, the *T&G Record*. Particularly, Morris focused on Beckett's criticism of the Tory industrial relations law reform and Blair's refusal to commit to repeal these measures.

Table 2: Labour Leadership Election 1994 – Result

		Affiliated [inc unions] (33.3%)		CLPs (33.3%)		PLP and EPLP (33.3%)		Overall result
		Votes	%	Votes	%	Votes	%	%
T.	Blair	407,637	52.3	100,313	58.2	198	60.5	57.0
J.	Prescott	221,367	28.4	42,053	24.4	64	19.6	24.1
M.	Beckett	150,422	19.3	29,990	17.4	65	19.9	18.9

The electoral college had not frozen the unions out as many on the right had hoped. Wickham-Jones stated: 'Margaret Beckett did not come first among members of the T&G that had supported her. But the 33.5 per cent she received was her best performance among any union … For unions, it was clear that public recommendations and formal support offered a means of intervention'.[5]

This was a point amplified in 2010 when union nominations and campaigning delivered Ed Miliband to the leadership over his brother David, who had won in the CLP and MP/MEP sections.

Blair and Shifting Labour to the Right

After his victory, Blair shocked the party by announcing at the subsequent Annual Conference that he intended to rewrite Clause IV of the party's constitution, specifically removing wording in support of nationalisation. This would mean that the party would no longer be committed to the public ownership of the commanding heights of the economy.

At the Special Labour Party Conference held in the spring 1995 the T&G (and Unison) prevented Blair achieving a total landslide in revising Clause IV, although the margin of victory was not in any way questionable. The Reuters report, picked up by the *New York Times*, reads:

Britain's two biggest unions, representing transport and public sector workers, voted against Mr Blair. But the overall union vote, accounting for 70 percent of the conference total, broke down 38 percent to 32 percent in his favour. Among rank and file members,

5 Wickham-Jones, 'Introducing OMOV', pp.45, 49.

who cast the remaining 30 percent of the vote, the margin was an overwhelming 27 percent to 3 percent.[6]

In his speech to the T&G's BDC in 1995, not a word was spoken about Clause IV. But in among the positive talk about the European Social Charter, the National Minimum Wage, restoration of union rights at Government Communications Headquarters (GCHQ) and ending triennial checkoff ballots, Blair put the unions on notice that things were going to change. He argued that Labour would govern in the interests of the whole country, which of course included employers, and so relegated the union voice to just one of any number of voices competing for a political hearing: 'the days when demands could be made of the Labour Party by trade unions which they could simply expect to be met were over and would not be coming back'.[7]

In this same speech, Blair took time out to praise the new members, trade union political levy payers, coming into the party. In retrospect this is not at all surprising; Robinson cites work that shows that these new members were precisely those who would support 'modernisation' and the Blair project more generally: 'new members were attracted to the Party because of its attempts to change … the post 1994 recruits were "significantly more likely to be modernisers" and "more trusting of the Party leadership" than people who had joined the Party before 1994'.[8]

At the 1996 TUC Congress, just in advance of that year's Labour Party Conference, Stephen Byers, a shadow minister in Labour's employment team, was overheard briefing lobby journalists, his key message being that it was now time for Labour to break its historic link with the unions.

Blair had no background in the labour movement and no empathy with unions and their members; although sponsored by the T&G, his principal purpose of membership was in using the union's Northern Regional Secretary to secure his adoption in the Sedgefield parliamentary constituency in County Durham. Sedgefield was well to the south of what was then still left of the Durham coalfield, ensuring no unhelpful intervention by recidivist miners.

Perhaps buoyed by the easy victory regarding Clause IV, the Blair cabal clearly believed that it was an opportune moment to move against the unions. He had only just managed to secure a majority in the union section on Clause IV, so removing this potential obstacle to the creation of a fully-fledged New Labour Party was a top priority.

The *Guardian* columnist Seamus Milne notes: 'Mr Blair himself has

6 Reuters, 'British Labor drops pledge on nationalization', *New York Times*, 30 April 1995.

7 Minutes of the Proceedings of the 36th Biennial Delegate Conference 1995.

8 E. Robinson, 'Recapturing Labour's traditions? History, nostalgia and the re-writing of Clause IV' (2007) www.psa.ac.uk/sites/default/files/243_256_0.pdf.

never made any secret in private of his view that the unions' constitutional role in the party is inappropriate for a modern political organisation. He argued that case openly in meetings with union leaders during Labour's last great constitutional spat over the unions' involvement in parliamentary selections in 1993'.[9]

Although this issue was not carried through to any conclusion, it remained a running sore for New Labour. Although outside the scope of this volume, we may note that the next crisis, albeit contrived, over the role of trade unions led to the Collins Review in 2014, which reformed many democratic procedures including the process for the election of the leader of the party. The unintended consequence of Collins was to allow for the surprise election of left of centre, and very much not New Labour, Jeremy Corbyn as leader of the party in 2015.

The mid-1990s is dealt with in great detail in Lewis Minkin's study of Blair's management and essential takeover of the Labour Party[10] including, once the Blairite takeover was complete, the accommodating role played by many union representatives on the National Executive Committee, including those from the T&G, a union apparently on the left of the political divide.

Labour as a 'Post-Social Democratic' Government

In the 1997 general election Blair led Labour to a landslide victory. Labour won 418 seats compared with 165 for the Tories and 46 for the Liberal Democrats. But it remains a moot point if the popular mood was *for* New Labour or *against* an increasingly sclerotic and corrupt Conservative government.

The Blair administration proceeded apace with an essentially neo-liberal, pro-business agenda of privatisation, outsourcing, and deregulation. Business leaders, not trade union leaders, were invited to join the government as key advisors. Milne states: 'There is no question that the crowning of New Labour represents a historic break. If the 1981 Mitterrand government can be seen as the last throw of the post-war reformist left the Blair administration is the first explicitly post-social-democratic government in a major Western state'.[11]

Although Foreign Secretary Robin Cook had signalled a move to an ethical foreign policy, by the early years of the new century Blair was

9 S. Milne, 'Disputed restaurant briefing signals end of historic link with Labour', *The Guardian*, 14 September 1996.

10 L. Minkin, *The Blair Supremacy: a Study in the Politics of Labour's Party Management* (Manchester University Press, 2014).

11 S. Milne, *The Revenge of History* (Verso, 2013), p.81.

clearly in the neo-conservative camp and a chief exponent of wars of liberal intervention.

Gordon Brown's light touch regulation of the City of London contributed to the financial crisis of 2008. New Labour's austerity measures were increasingly seen as Tory lite. It came as a surprise to nobody that Labour, after 13 years in office pursuing a neo-liberal agenda, lost the 2010 general election to a Tory–Liberal coalition with more of the same, and it some cases worse, to come.

The Labour Government and Trade Union Rights

From 1980 the Conservative government enacted a succession of anti-union laws that negatively interfered with a union's right to organise strike action, how it polled its members on such action, how it set about picketing, how it may seek to extend the action and how it should elect its executive committee and principal officers.[12] The principal purpose of these new laws was twofold: to limit the extent to which unions were able to win for existing members at work; and to limit unions' ability to organise new members into the union.

Other than giving each successive Secretary of State the opportunity to show the Tory faithful and the Prime Minister how tough he or she was in dealing with the unions, there was also a more rational purpose in introducing these laws on a piecemeal basis. The new arrangements under Thatcher and Major did not repeat earlier errors; new laws were successively introduced that progressively cut away unions' rights. Further there was no new court established, employers and dissident union members could enforce their new rights through the existing courts, mainly by application for injunctive relief.

As the 1980s turned into the 1990s it was not at all apparent that Labour would seek to repeal these laws when in government. Labour leader Neil Kinnock established a policy review in the late 1980s. The most important paper to emerge from the review, from the unions' point of view, was *Looking to the Future* in 1990. 'Agreements were sought with the unions on matters such as picketing restrictions and the abolition of the closed shop. *Looking to the Future* made it clear that the unions would not be given back the powers they had enjoyed in the 1970s'.[13] This was confirmed in the 1992 Labour manifesto, which proposed no change on the law on picketing or closed shops.

The T&G, as witnessed at the 33rd BDC held in 1989, was moving

---

12 See J. McIlroy, *The Permanent Revolution? Conservative Law and the Trade Unions* (Spokesman, 1991).

13 M. Bevir, 'The remaking of Labour, 1987–1997', *Observatoire de la société britannique*, 2009, p.7.

in the opposite direction to Labour's policy review. Composite Motion 42 read: 'Conference welcomes the Labour Party's 1988 Conference decision to campaign for a major extension of individual employment rights for all workers; and calls for a repeal of all anti-trade union legislation and opposes attempts to interfere in the union's rule book'.[14]

The union recognised that a simple call for repeal was not in itself sufficient; what was necessary was a parallel package of rights and freedoms for workers and unions. But Labour's new thinking was that while individual rights at work may be acceptable, collective rights exercised through the unions should not be given consideration.

The 35th BDC held in 1993, although giving up on relying on the pro-union Labour Conference decision of 1988, again called, in Composite 8, for the repeal of the anti-union laws and for a new package of individual and collective rights at work: 'Conference calls for the repeal of all anti-trade union laws and their replacement with a positive framework of individual and collective rights at work'.[15]

Blair was a keynote speaker at the 36th BDC in 1995. His speech dealt with many of the employment rights issues that were acceptable and would be legislated for; but on the question of trade union rights he was silent. He may have been silent, but the conference was not, Composite 5 called for repeal and a new framework of rights and freedoms: 'This Conference calls for the next Labour Government to repeal all anti-union laws on assuming office and replace them by a framework of guaranteed rights and freedoms'.[16]

In 1996, one of the new-look Blairite Labour Party committees was tasked with working on the pre-manifesto document *Building Prosperity, Flexibility and Fairness at Work*. The outcome was an acceptance that the anti-union laws of the Thatcher/Major period were here to stay. Even the limited 1993 reform offered by the late leader, John Smith, whose place Blair had taken, of rights from the first day of employment, not to be unfairly dismissed – so no qualifying period – was dropped.

But as Minkin notes:

[A] range of positive commitments did appeal to the unions. Britain would be part of the European social chapter. The staff at GCHQ would regain the right to belong to an independent trade union. There would be a legal obligation to recognise a trade union. Employers would be encouraged to develop family friendly policies. There would be procedures for information and adequate consultation and the right to present a claim for unfair dismissal

14 Minutes of the Proceedings of the 33rd Biennial Delegate Conference 1989, p.48.
15 Minutes of the Proceedings of the 35th Biennial Delegate Conference 1993, p.22.
16 Minutes of the Proceedings of the 36th Biennial Delegate Conference 1995, p.35.

where industrial action had been lawful, with the right also to be accompanied at disciplinary or grievance procedure meetings.[17]

The Queen's Speech on 14 May 1997 contained most of these early commitments, which had indeed made it through to the manifesto, together with a further commitment to the National Minimum Wage. The Secretary of State for implementing much of this was to be Margaret Beckett, but she was soon replaced by Peter Mandelson, someone who did not inspire the confidence of the trade unions.

The T&G was not to be won over to the idea of dropping its quest for trade union rights. The 37th BDC in July 1997 again persisted with its central demand of repeal and a new framework of all-encompassing labour rights. Composite 12 read: 'this Conference calls on the new Government to repeal all anti-union laws and to adopt a framework of labour law conforming to standards set by the International Labour Organisation and the United Nations Declaration of Human Rights ... Conference commends the work of the Institute of Employment Rights'.[18]

Under Beckett's nominal control, in Spring 1998 a White Paper entitled *Fairness at Work* was published, setting out in more detail the general pledges made in the previous year. There had been clear backtracking as a result of business lobbying, to the extent that Bill Morris gave the White Paper 'two cheers only'. The business-friendly Mandelson took over from Beckett in July 1998 as the White Paper became the Employment Relations Bill, with additional pressures to dilute further the provisions as set out in the Queen's Speech and the White Paper. When the Bill was published just before Christmas, the headline features were often subject to qualification. The family-friendly proposals were uncontroversial but clearly, as had always been promised, there was no movement on the 1980s Thatcher/Major anti-union legislation.

A dispute broke out at Heathrow in November 1998, at LSG Skychefs, an airline catering contractor and part of a multinational joint venture involving particularly Lufthansa, the German national flag carrier. 270 T&G members objecting to changes to working practices took two days' strike action and were promptly dismissed. Although the union responded using some tactics not tried before, including picketing the German embassy – an early example of leverage – the strike was not resolved until April 2000 with compensation payments running into several thousand pounds but no reinstatements.

At this early stage in the life of the Labour government it was clear that, for all of Bill Morris' quiet diplomacy with the Labour leadership,

---

17 Minkin, *The Blair Supremacy*, p.278.
18 Minutes of the Proceedings of the 37th Biennial Delegate Conference 1997, pp.12–13.

Blair and Mandelson had no interest in intervening on behalf of the LSG Skychef workers and, in the bigger picture, no interest at all in repealing the anti-union laws introduced under Thatcher and Major.

Gordon Brown, Chancellor of the Exchequer, was the keynote speaker at the 38th BDC in 1999. Brown's address touched on what New Labour saw as its positive employment rights package: 'the New Labour government was also delivering on statutory rights which included, the right to be a member of a trade union, as at GCHQ, and the right to have a trade union to negotiate for them, as well as proper compensation against unfair dismissal. They had also signed the Social Chapter and the Working Time Directive'.[19]

Brown was, of course, not wrong to highlight these points; New Labour had promised very modest reforms to employment law and what was being delivered was indeed very modest.

Composite 19 very diplomatically welcomed such progress that had been made by the Labour government, but kept up the demand for repeal and a new package of positive rights:

> Conference welcomes the many positive steps taken by the Labour Government over the last two years to redress the balance of workplace relations and to promote social justice at work ... The continued restrictions placed on British workers are both contrary to fairness at work and the stated aim of the Labour Government to create a fairer society. This is particularly evident from the plight of the Skychef workers ... who received no protection from the legislation ...Conference also believes that the T&G, in conjunction with TUC affiliates and other labour organisations, should ... campaign vigorously for:

- a framework of labour law conforming to standards set by the International Labour Organisation and the United Nations Declaration of Human Rights
- the repeal of the anti-union laws.[20]

It was now clear that the union and the Party were, if not drifting apart, not able to come together on the question of trade union rights. Although Labour legislated further on labour rights with the Employment Act 2002, it failed to address the issue that had been T&G policy since at least the 33rd BDC in 1989 – the repeal of anti-union laws and their replacement with a new framework of positive rights and freedoms.

19 Minutes of the Proceedings of the 38th Biennial Delegate Conference 1999, p.10.
20 Minutes of the Proceedings of the 38th Biennial Delegate Conference 1999, pp.48–49.

Figure 4: Gate
Gourmet
pickets,
Heathrow
Airport, 2005

This remained the T&G's position through the 39th BDC (2001), the 40th BDC (2003) – Tony Woodley's first as General Secretary, the 41st BDC (2005), and the 42nd and final BDC (2007).

A dispute at another airline caterer, Gate Gourmet, at Heathrow in 2005 allowed Woodley to win a rare victory at Labour Party Conference, winning a vote committing the party to improve labour rights in the UK. The *Times* newspaper noted

[T]rade unions voted last night to inflict an embarrassing defeat on Tony Blair by committing the Labour conference to demand the legalisation of secondary strike action … The T&G union, which last night appeared to have settled its long-running dispute with the Gate Gourmet catering company, led calls to reintroduce 'solidarity action'. That came after a secondary strike by British Airways staff that brought flights at Heathrow to a halt in the summer in support of workers dismissed by Gate Gourmet.[21]

21 D. Charter, 'Unions inflict defeat on Blair over secondary strike action', *The Times*, 27 September 2005.

Of course, in keeping with tradition, the party leadership ignored inconvenient policy carried at Conference.

With the publication in 1998 of the White Paper *Fairness at Work*, which eventually became the Employment Relations Act 1999, Tony Blair said: 'The changes that we do propose would leave British law the most restrictive on trade unions in the Western world'. In this he was true to his word; during his premiership and under Brown's that followed there was never any question that Labour would veer from this position.

Devolved Assemblies: Northern Ireland, Scotland, Wales and London

Labour was committed to devolution from at least its general election defeat in 1992. Leader John Smith's pledge to devolution was set out at the 35th BDC in 1993. In his address to Conference the minutes record him pledging 'new tiers of government in Scotland and Wales and in the regions of England'.[22]

In 1998 devolved institutions in Scotland, Wales and Northern Ireland were established. In the case of Northern Ireland the devolution of executive power was not new – although mandatory cross-community power-sharing, based on an assembly elected by proportional representation, was indeed an important new development.

In all cases, in Scotland, Wales and Northern Ireland, the new parliamentary institutions possessed, at least on paper, significant powers over economic and social policy. In each case the trade union movement had played an important, often key, role in creating the conditions for their establishment – and, within this, the T&G (and the union's Irish wing, the ATGWU (Amalgamated Transport & General Workers Union)) was a leading player.

In a period of radical deindustrialisation, when both Conservative and Labour policy at Westminster was dominated by neo-liberal, pro-big business perspectives, trade unionists in all three jurisdictions and in London saw local powers of public sector intervention, backed by a democratic mandate, as increasingly critical.

Northern Ireland: Devolution, Class Politics and an Unfinished Peace Process
John Foster
Here, however, the similarities largely end. Unlike the new institutions in Scotland and Wales, the establishment of the Northern Ireland Assembly followed 30 years of acute civil and military conflict – conflict that had

22 Minutes of the Proceedings of the 35th Biennial Delegate Conference 1993, p.38.

posed very particular challenges to the trade union movement. The 1998 Good Friday Agreement, which established the new Assembly, represented a significant, though not conclusive, step in resolving the most violent manifestations of this conflict and, in order to understand the union's role at this stage, it is important to understand the long-term nature of ATGWU's contribution.[23]

In the 1950s and 1960s it had been the ATGWU's Regional Secretary, Norman Kennedy, who had played a major role in recreating a united Irish trade union movement, first the united all-Ireland Irish Congress of Trades Unions (ICTU) and then setting up its Northern Ireland Committee (NIC ICTU). Kennedy had also been a significant advocate within the Northern Ireland Labour Party in giving support to moves for an equality of civil rights in the North and for dismantling the systematic discrimination – in voting rights and access to housing, employment and education – that had historically sustained Unionist control in the six counties.[24] Individual members of the ATGWU, often themselves leading officials, had helped staff the Northern Ireland Civil Rights Association, which, from 1965, had sought to create – with some success – a broad, cross-community movement to secure an equality of basic rights. It had also been ATGWU members, often as officers of Belfast and other trades councils, who had sought to defend this movement against growing sectarian pressures on both sides and, after 1970, from coercive action by the British government. The names of two ATGWU members, Betty Sinclair and Joe Cooper, respectively Secretary and Chair of Belfast Trades Council, stand out.[25]

However, the major contribution of the trade union movement in Northern Ireland, and of the ATGWU as its biggest component, was of a different kind, one that was less visible but more profound: the practical operation of non-sectarian trade unionism across Northern Ireland.

Despite the scale of unemployment, the North had one of the highest levels of trade union density anywhere in the two islands. In the 1960s Northern Ireland still had significant employment in its traditional industries – heavy engineering, shipbuilding, textiles and food – and also in the new incoming plants in electronics, synthetics, rubber, computing

---

23 The narrative for Ireland is based on the surviving minutes and policy documents in the ATGWU/Unite offices in Antrim Road, Belfast and on interviews with Joe Bowers, previous president of the NI Confed, Peter Bunting, former AGS NIC ICTU, Kevin Cooper, Convener of the Trade Union group in the NI Civic Forum 1999–2002, Maurice Cunningham (ATGWU officer), Eugene McGlone, former Deputy Regional Secretary ATGWU and Mick O'Reilly, former Regional Secretary ATGWU.
24 T. Cradden, 'Trade union movement in Northern Ireland' in D. Nevin, *Trade Union Century* (Mercier Press, 1994); Charles McCarthy, *Trade Unions in Ireland* (Dublin Institute of Public Administration, 1977).
25 Madge Davidson, *We Shall Overcome: a History of the Struggle for Civil Right in Northern Ireland 1968–1978* (republished by Belfast and District Trades Council, 2019).

and avionics. In most of these industries, though not all, Catholics and Protestants were employed within the same workplaces even if sometimes in different departments and at different grades. As workers, both Protestant and Catholic, they therefore identified with, and were active in, the same unions and, by necessity, collectively defended their jobs, conditions and remuneration. And they did so, as measured by strike activity, at a higher level than their fellow workers across the sea in Britain.[26]

The resulting trade union identities were therefore very significant. By their nature, embracing solidarity with fellow workers, they were distinct from, and in some ways in conflict with, those that operated within Northern Ireland's highly segregated communities. Here religious, political and paramilitary organisations exercised a controlling discipline and did so, as measured by housing segregation, to an increasing degree as sectarian violence continued largely unabated into the twenty-first century.

As Peter Bunting, then Assistant General Secretary of ICTU with responsibility for the Northern Ireland Committee stresses, it was these employment relations – embodied in real people and in their courage and comradeship across sectarian boundaries – that provided the wider basis for the non-sectarian political influence of the trade union movement. Sectarian organisations tried but never fully succeeded in overcoming this workplace-based solidarity. In 1974 the Ulster Defence Association, as part of its successful attempt to bring down the power-sharing Executive in the North, organised a paramilitary blockade of workplaces. Afterwards, the same forces made a determined attempt to break trade union influence and assert that of an 'Ulster Workers Association'.[27] Demands were made for the ejection of shop stewards and union officers who did not recognise its authority. These demands secured virtually no response, despite significant paramilitary intimidation. Workers, both Catholic and Protestant, returned to their employment and continued to give their support to their pre-existing shop stewards and trade unions.

It is important also to stress that this was no mere passive reaction on the part of the trade union movement and its leaders. During the lockout itself, union and workplace leaders had directly challenged the paramilitaries – with Norman Kennedy and Andy Holmes, convener at Harland and Wolff, leading a defiant march back to work.[28] Over

26 TGWU General Executive Committee Minutes, Disputes for 1968,1969, 1970 and 1971, Minutes of the ATGWU Quarterly, January, April, July 1971 (Unite Offices, Antrim Road, Belfast). Emmet O'Connor, *Labour History of Ireland 1824–2000* (University College Dublin Press, 2011), pp. 275–276.

27 *Newsletter*, 12 August 1974; Leaflet under the name J. Best (Trade Union Box, Belfast Linenhall Library); Ben Segal, 'Irish trade unions – working for peace in Northern Ireland', *Labor Studies Journal*, 1977–78, vol.3, no.2.

28 Robert Fisk, *The Times*, 12 August 1974.

the following months the NIC ICTU – in part at the initiative of the ATGWU's new Regional Secretary John Freeman – also responded strategically. It gave organisational priority to the redevelopment of the wider community base of the trade union movement through a network of trades councils across the whole of the North. As trades councils, these bodies had the capability to bring together different unions on a locality basis in order to make collective demands on behalf of people locally, whatever their religious affiliation.[29] By 1976–1977 well over a dozen new or revived trades councils were in operation. By then, also, NIC ICTU had launched the *Better Life for All* campaign, with mass meetings in town and city centres demanding jobs and services on behalf of all people across the North.[30] That year, in July 1977, Unionist politician Ian Paisley made another attempt at a lockout. This one, however, had to be abandoned. Trade union members across Northern Ireland defied the paramilitaries – some paying for it with their lives – and basic services, such as transport and food distribution, were maintained.

These years in the late 1970s probably marked the peak of this wider community influence – with union membership at its height, joint action against the wage freezes of the Callaghan government followed by even bigger mobilisations against the hard-line policies of the incoming Conservatives. 1980 saw NIC ICTU organising mass rallies in central Belfast with contingents marching in from every area of the city to united demonstrations of class solidarity.

Soon, however, the material impact of Conservative policies made itself felt. By 1981 unemployment had reached 20 per cent, and by 1986 industrial employment, so important for consolidating wider trade union identities, had collapsed by over a third – dropping from 172,000 to just 103,000. With it, ATGWU membership also declined sharply – as did levels of industrial action. This fell from previously well above that in Britain to well below it. The activity of trades councils declined, a number went out of existence and even Belfast saw its attendance only partly maintained by the increase in delegates from public sector unions.[31]

So, in terms of the relationship between workplace and community identities, the balance once more shifted in a sectarian direction. As the number of deaths from civil and military conflict moved up from 2,000 to over 3,000, housing segregation across the province increased. While public sector employment did grow somewhat, it did not compensate for the loss of industrial jobs and was generally in areas, such as security or servicing local communities, that did not cross sectarian boundaries.

29 ATGWU Regional Committee Minutes, 5–6 January 1975.
30 Terry Carlin, Northern Ireland Officer of ICTU, Address to ICTU Trades Council Conference Annual Seminar, Bray 1977.
31 The evidence is reviewed in Volume 5 of this series.

The ATGWU response, in terms of maintaining its campaigning against sectarianism and sectarian violence, was to focus on more targeted initiatives – using the union's active links within working class communities, both Catholic and Protestant, to develop dialogues across the sectarian divide. In particular it sought to involve paramilitary organisations, all of which, to a greater or less extent, claimed working class political credentials and drew their recruits from working class communities. In 1983 the union backed the creation of the People's College in Belfast and, over the same period, helped finance the Belfast Unemployed Workers Centre, which, based in the non-sectarian territory of central Belfast, drew together campaigners from both sides of the religious divide. From 1988 the union contributed to the establishment of CounterAct, which, in particular, sought to build links with and between the different sectarian communities. Joe Law, an ATGWU member from a Protestant background, played an important role, as did another TGWU member, Brenda Callaghan – one among the many women who represented the peace movement within, and across, working class communities.[32]

One of the most important of the associated organisations was what became the Messines Fellowship, convened by Joe Bowers, President of the Confederation of Shipbuilding and Engineering Workers in Northern Ireland and who, as a Northern Ireland officer for MSF, represented workers in Harland and Wolff and the Shorts aircraft factory. Messines had been a First World War battle in which both Catholic and Protestant volunteers from Ireland suffered heavy casualties. The association's regular meetings were attended by representatives of the Provisional IRA, the Officials, the Progressive Unionist Part and the Ulster Volunteer Force, the Ulster Political Research Group and the Ulster Defence Association, the Irish National Liberation Army and the Irish Republican Socialist Party.[33]

Most of those attending were trade union members whose organisations, though sectarian, included in their programmes left-wing or socialist objectives, and did so in contrast to, and often in conflict with, elite controlled organisations rooted in the Unionist ascendancy, the evangelical churches or, conversely, Catholic orthodoxy. Trade union calls for employment, better housing and welfare services converged with the slogans by which the paramilitaries sustained their own local bases of support.

The determination with which ATGWU leaders in the North, led by John Freeman, condemned the privatising, neo-liberal policies of the Conservative governments in the 1990s reflected this understanding – as did, from 1997, their opposition to the very similar policies of the successor New Labour government. They knew that any progress in establishing

---

32 Brian Campfield (ed.), 'Essays in honour of Joe Law', special issue *of Social Justice Review* (Trademark, 2017).
33 Joe Bowers, Interview April 2022 (Unite Oral History Archive).

dialogue could only be sustained by an active public commitment to defend Northern Ireland's working class from the worsening impact of job loss and deindustrialisation.

Through the 1990s, the peace process lurched from temporary ceasefires to renewed and sometimes deepening violence. The Belfast Trades Union Council annual reports for 1991 and 1992 describe sectarian conflict as escalating.[34] The Quarterly Meeting of the ATGWU Committee for January 1992 had to be delayed because of bombing in central Belfast. It then heard representatives of the Bakers branch call for renewed anti-sectarian initiatives in face of a near-lethal attempt on the life of the shop steward convener at the giant Ormeau bakery. Pearce McKenna had sought the implementation of new regulations against sectarian flags in the workplace. He was shot down outside.[35] Later meetings of the ATGWU heard calls for increased resources for anti-sectarian activity and proposals for broad campaigns against the imposition of compulsory competitive tendering and the privatisation of the water supply and of Belfast airport. In 1993 the ATGWU welcomed the new NIC ICTU initiative for 'Peace Work and Progress' and provided much of the funding for it. Mass rallies across the North combined economic demands with the call for peace and, at least in part, provided the context for the Downing Street agreement of December 1993 and ceasefires by both the IRA and the Combined Loyalist Command in 1994.

But 1995 and 1996 again saw reverse developments, with the Conservative government now dependent on Ulster Unionist votes in the Commons. The IRA and loyalists ended their ceasefires and both Ian Paisley's Democratic Unionist Party and David Trimble's Ulster Unionist Party sought to reassert their own populist support by backing provocative Orange Order marches through Catholic areas. The Belfast Trades Council reports for 1996 and 1997 noted the close links between the collapse of peace hopes, the deteriorating economic situation and cuts to the public sector supported, in the form of the 'worst type of bipartisanship', by the new Labour leadership of Tony Blair. The ATGWU officer responsible for textiles, Maurice Cunningham, remembers a resurgence of sectarian conflict in and around workplaces at the same time as the North's remaining textile factories continued to close.[36] NIC ICTU, the ATGWU and Belfast Trades Council responded by intensifying dialogue with paramilitaries around attempts to develop a common economic agenda to defend working class communities.[37]

34 Annual Reports, Belfast Trades Union Council, Linenhall Library Belfast, Political Collection.

35 ATGWU Quarterly Meeting Minutes, January 1992 (Antrim Road, Belfast).

36 Maurice Cunningham interviewed May 2022 (Unite Oral History Archive).

37 This summary is mainly based on the annual reports of Belfast and District Trades Union Council 1990–1998.

It was a combination of these renewed discussions with the paramilitaries, the intervention by Senator George Mitchell with the IRA and the election of a Labour government with Mo Mowlam as Secretary of State for Northern Ireland that finally brought about the Belfast Agreement of 10 April 1998 – and, with it, a consensus on the need for new power-sharing devolved institutions.

This marked a critical turning point. But it was, as it proved, a limited and precarious one. Those leading the trade union movement, and the civil society movements for peace, understood that any secure progress depended on addressing the fundamental issues of economic and social injustice as experienced across the North's working class communities – problems that were becoming more and not less entrenched. The inclusion of a Civic Forum in the devolution proposals sought to meet this need and to provide representation for those organisations that, in terms of activity in working class communities, had played a central role in the peace process but were unlikely to have a significant voice in the Assembly itself. These included working class based parties with links to paramilitaries, such as the Progressive Unionist Party, and cross-community organisations such as the Women's Coalition led by ATGWU members Monica McWilliams and May Blood.[38] Mo Mowlam stressed this potential role of the Civic Assembly to 'speak for the working class and especially the working class women of Northern Ireland' when presenting these two ATGWU members with the T&G's Frank Cousins Peace Award in June 1999. 'The unions will have a bigger role to play in the future of the Civic Forum, helping to develop policy for the future'.[39]

The newly appointed Regional Secretary of ATGWU, Mick O'Reilly, previously an ATGWU officer based in the Republic of Ireland, strongly backed the Civic Forum and became a member – one of seven – of the trade union group convened by Kevin Cooper.[40] O'Reilly understood that real progress towards peace could only be realised by active, united campaigning in defence of working class interests across the North's divided communities. This meant challenging the neo-liberal policies of the Blair government – which soon saw the members of the Civic Assembly clashing with Mo Mowlam's successor as Secretary of State, Peter Mandelson. In one famous exchange, during a frustrating visit to Stormont Castle, Monica McWilliams told Blair's pro-consul, at the time

38 Civic Forum, Trade Union Group papers as held by its Convener Kevin Cooper, Unite Offices, Antrim Road Belfast: Response to Programme for Growth, 15 June 2000.
39 TGWU Record, June 1999.
40 Mick O'Reilly, *From Lucifer to Lazarus* (Lilliput Press, 2019) p.140; interview with Mick O'Reilly April 2022.

lounging with his feet up on a historic table, that his best way of helping would be 'to take your feet off *our* table and get back to England'.[41]

These tensions – between New Labour and a working class agenda – were soon felt within the TGWU at British level. At the 1999 BDC O'Reilly came into conflict with the General Secretary Bill Morris by insisting that, with the Good Friday Agreement in place, the time had come for a substantive debate on Ireland.[42] This had to include issues raised by Irish branches condemning the neo-liberal policies of the Blair administration and calling for, among other things, active campaigning against the attempted privatisation of Northern Ireland's water, against the imposition of compulsory competitive tendering and the private partner-ship initiative, the need for a real policy role for the Civic Assembly, and consideration of sensitive issues such as the rights of the Irish language. In doing so, O'Reilly was voicing the concerns of the union's Irish BDC the year before.[43] This had passed an emergency motion to support all pro-agreement parties in the referendum to 'create an Assembly where a progressive coalition of political representatives can be created to advance the interests of working people' and 'an inclusive dialogue with all sections of the community'. The 1998 Irish BDC had then passed a series of resolu-tions that called for a reversal of Labour's neo-liberal policies and pledged support for the Liverpool dockers in their fight against the loss of jobs.

The following year, 2000, the Irish BDC maintained its demands for a change of course: opposition to the privatisation of Belfast harbour, to the deregulation of Northern Ireland's buses and to new regulations for the use of agency labour. It did so in the knowledge that peace in Northern Ireland depended on maintaining the momentum of hope in working class communities, both Catholic and Protestant, that new political institutions could improve material conditions and halt continued deterioration.[44] The Civic Forum, though producing a major report on poverty, had found itself sidelined with little or no input into policy. Then, amidst rising sectarian tensions, the power-sharing Assembly was itself suspended in October 2002 when the unionist parties walked out. The Assembly remained suspended till 2007.

A few months before its suspension, in summer 2001, Mick O'Reilly had himself been suspended from office, along with the ATGWU Deputy Regional Secretary Eugene McGlone. They were then dismissed by

41 Interview with Eugene McGlone, former Deputy General Secretary ATGWU April 2022.
42 Mick O'Reilly, *Lucifer*, pp.139–140; BDC 1999 report: motions from Irish branches 3/38, 3/83.
43 Report of the ATGWU 1998 Biennial, motions from branches 3/90/ 3/14, 3/364 and Emergency Resolution.
44 Irish Biennial Delegate Conference, 16 June 2000: Motions from 3/15, 3/16/ 3/105, 3/8 (Unite, Antrim Road).

General Secretary Bill Morris, despite full backing by the ATGWU Executive in Ireland. Three years later a further investigation after the election of Tony Woodley found no evidence at all of wrong-doing. Both were reinstated.

However, their earlier dismissal had, for a three-year period, removed from the North's biggest union two key figures committed to progressive policies at a key juncture in the peace process. The union was largely immobilised. Over the same period Joe Bowers, President of the Confederation of Shipbuilding and Engineering Unions and a key figure in the dialogue with paramilitaries, was, along with a number of shop stewards at Shorts, also removed from their union positions by the New Labour-supporting leader of MSF. Bowers had over previous months been leading resistance to the transfer of 2,000 high-tech posts in Shorts aircraft factory to Canada, in a deal with the new private owners, Bombardier, that had been sanctioned by the Blair government. Shorts traditionally provided major employment for Protestant East Belfast.[45]

The Northern Ireland Assembly was, temporarily, restored in 2007. But there was now no Civic Assembly. Political formations representing progressive politics, such as the Women's Coalition, failed to secure election and the Progressive Unionist Party was reduced to one seat, held by Dawn Purvis. The momentum of practical class politics, with its potential for building cross-community unity, had, over these critical years, been significantly weakened – a weakening that resulted both from the continuing loss of jobs and trade union membership, but also from political interventions in the movement itself.

The restored leadership of the ATGWU resumed its previous policies, with its progressive direction soon strengthened by the creation of Unite. But it now had to do so in significantly more difficult circumstances. The hopes of 1997–1998 had been that organisations based in working class areas, whether cross-community, such as the Women's Coalition, or working class-based organisations, such as the Progressive Unionist Party could – in the context of mass trade union campaigning on issues of poverty, unemployment and deindustrialisation – shift the balance of mass politics in Northern Ireland. Instead, by 2007 parties representing the sectarian elites had fully resecured their positions – making any stable power-sharing administration extremely problematic.

---

45 Interviews with Mick O'Reilly, Eugene McGlone and Joe Bowers in April 2022 and Pat Stuart, then a TGWU Executive member, in May 2022 (Unite Oral History Archive). For details of the removal of Joe Bowers and the Shorts shop stewards: *Bowers v Amicus (MSF)*, Fair Employment Tribunal, 10 December 2007; and the *Belfast Telegraph*, 4 July 2008 reporting the eventual legal overturning of the actions against the shop stewards taken in 1999–2000 by the then MSF General Secretary.

Devolution in Scotland: Another Politically Unfinished Process
John Foster

In the 1960s and 1970s it was the Scottish trade union movement that pushed the issue of Scottish devolution to the front of the Scotland's political agenda.[46] In 1968 the Scottish miners placed the demand for a parliament on the order paper of the Scottish Trades Union Congress (STUC) and it was the TGWU, among other unions, that ensured it became STUC policy in 1969.[47] Three years later, in February 1972 at the height of the crisis in Scottish shipbuilding, it was the STUC that convened the first Scottish Assembly and, with the support of the great bulk of Scottish local authorities and the organised working class movement, demanded locally determined powers of intervention in Scotland's economy.[48] In 1974–1975, with the Tories chased from power, it was Alex Kitson, as both Assistant General Secretary of the TGWU and an officer of the Labour Party, who successfully led the fight for this to become Labour Party policy. And when the Scottish referendum of 1978 failed to secure a sufficiently large majority for devolution, it was Kitson in the Labour Party and Hugh Wyper in the TGWU, along with Jimmy Milne and his successors Campbell Christie and Bill Speirs at the STUC, who revived the momentum of the campaign – both in Scotland United and its successor organisation, the Campaign for a Scottish Assembly.

Yet *The Story of the Scottish Parliament: the first two decades explained,* published by Edinburgh University Press in 2019, contains not one mention of the trade union movement.[49] Even in Brian Taylor's *Scottish Parliament*, also published by Edinburgh University Press but much earlier in 2002, trade unions and the STUC are totally absent.[50] Taylor, as the BBC's Scottish political correspondent, deploys a cast of thousands. Not one person is mentioned in connection with the trade union movement. Professor Michael Keating's 2010 *The Government of Scotland: public policy making after devolution* does mention trade unions – but just once. It is their *absence*, he says, that at least partially explains the sudden dominance in Scotland in the post-2000 period of the New Labour concepts of partnership and 'joined-up government' – which emerged in a 'period of sustained

---

46   This section is informed by interviews with Jane McKay, Yvonne Strachan TGWU Scotland's Women's Officer to 1999, Jackson Cullinane, Pat Stuart and Dave Moxham.

47   Lindsay Paterson, *A Diverse Assembly: the debate on a Scottish Parliament* (Edinburgh University Press, 1998) p.79 ff. provides key documents including the 1974 Annual Report of the Scottish Trades Union Congress, which reproduces documentation from 1968 and 1969.

48   Ray MacDonald, Scottish TGWU Secretary, was then chair of the STUC and led much of the discussion.

49   G. Hassan (ed.), *The Story of the Scottish Parliament: the First Two Decades Explained* (Edinburgh University Press, 2019).

50   Brian Taylor, *Scotland's Parliament* (Edinburgh University Press, 2002).

economic stability [...], the transformation of the economy to services, the demise of trade unions [...] and a new business elite based in financial services'.[51] Bill Speirs himself, as General Secretary of the STUC, told a fringe meeting at the 2001 TUC Conference: 'we are in danger of marginalisation from the democratic body we fought to secure, not because MSPs seek to exclude us but because we simply do not have the resources to take advantage of the opportunities that are there'. He mentions MSPs hardly finding 'space to move' for well-briefed representatives of big companies.[52]

There are, therefore, parallels with Northern Ireland. In both Ireland and Scotland, the trade union movement, and particularly the TGWU, had played a transformative role in the 1960s, 1970s and 1980s. But while individual trade union leaders had continued to play an important part thereafter, the wider movement lacked its previous force. This decline was organisational in terms of size and coherence. But probably still more important was a necessary consequence: the ability of the trade union movement to mobilise for, and indeed enforce, as Keating noted, an alternative class perspective to that of big business.

This was despite the fact that the form and character of the Scottish Parliament largely derived from earlier interventions by the trade union movement and particularly the TGWU. When we look today at the way in which the Scottish Parliament transacts its business, a very great deal can be traced back to the Campaign for a Scottish Assembly and, within this, to the STUC and particularly its Women's Committee.[53] The proposed electoral system, the call for 50:50 representation of women, the times of sittings and the length of sessions, the central consultative role of the committee system, the power of the Petitions Committee to propose legislation and the circular debating chamber with its stress on consensus, all reflect the recommendations of the STUC Women's Committee back in 1989. It was in fact Bill Speirs who, in 1998, drafted the detailed regulations for the new parliament's committee system.[54] The only recommendation that has totally fallen by the wayside was the proposal for a wider Civic Forum 'to represent the interests of civil society'. This, though temporarily funded, 'later atrophied', as Professor Keating puts it.[55]

Nor can there be any doubt that these structures facilitated the

51 Michael Keating, *The Government of Scotland: Public Policy Making after Devolution* (Edinburgh, 2010).

52 Bill Speirs speaking at a fringe meeting on regional devolution, reported in the *Morning Star*, 14 September 2001.

53 Interviews with Yvonne Strachan and Jane McKay; the August 1989 Report by Alice Brown and Yvonne Strachan is reproduced in Lindsay Paterson, *A Diverse Assembly*, pp.192–193.

54 Bill Speirs' partner, Pat Stuart, then a TGWU executive member, did the detailed copy-editing.

55 Keating, *The Government of Scotland*, p.33.

passage of some socially important legislation. In 2005 Elaine Smith MSP commended the provision of free bus travel for the elderly, free personal care, breakfast clubs for nursery and school children, the ending of university fees and the abolition of warrant sales.[56] Yet she also criticised opening aspects of the NHS to the private sector, the continued privatisation of housing, the use of PFI for public sector contracts and the lack of any overall strategy for economic and industrial development other than reliance on the private sector. Yvonne Strachan equally contrasts the pioneering work of the parliament on equalities and social justice with its failure to enact a progressive economic agenda.[57]

By the early 2000s the annual conferences of the STUC clearly reveal the rising dissatisfaction of delegates. New Labour priorities, if not explicit, clearly dominated the thinking of the new Lib–Lab coalition. This was manifest in the new Scottish government's refusal to intervene industrially to save threatened jobs – as in the Clyde shipyards in 2001 – its enforcement of housing stock transfer, its failure to restore publicly owned transport and its lack of any public sector strategy for industry.[58] In 1999 the TGWU Regional Secretary, Jimmy Elsby, along with Cathy Jamieson MSP (one of several supported by the TGWU), made an abortive call for the Lib–Lab administration to back publicly owned housing. The following year, Elsby was part of an equally abortive delegation to Donald Dewar, as First Minister, to persuade the Scottish government 'against its intention to transfer housing to private community-based organisations'.

In April 2002, and addressing some of its General Secretary's concerns, the STUC was able to announce that a memorandum of understanding had been negotiated with Scottish government and its then leader Jack McConnell. This laid down an intent to facilitate consultation on policy – although the scope of the memorandum was in practice quite limited and only guaranteed one meeting a year. In 2003, as Bill Speirs at the STUC led opposition to the invasion of Iraq, relations with the Scottish government again cooled.[59]

So here, in terms of devolved institutions, we have at least one partial parallel to Northern Ireland. In Ireland the new institutions of 1998–1999 might have embodied the momentum of the trade union and class-based

56 Elaine Smith MSP, later Deputy Convener of the Scottish Parliament, writing in V. Mills (ed.), *The Red Paper on Scotland* (Glasgow Caledonian University, 2005), pp.14–28.
57 Yvonne Strachan interview, 5 May 2022 (Unite Oral History Archive).
58 Reports of debates at the STUC conference in the *Morning Star*, 19 and 20 April 1999, that set out the expectations of trade unionists immediately prior to the Scottish Parliament elections and subsequently, in *the Morning Star*, 18 and 20 April 2000, covering the STUC for 2000 their disquiet and subsequently their discontent at the 2002 STUC (*Morning Star*, 20 April 2002).
59 David Moxham, Deputy General Secretary, STUC, notes the increasing divergence (interview Unite Oral History Archive June 2021).

politics as developed through the late 1970s and early 1980s – and in the 1990s of the local cross-community organisations reflecting and sustained by these same politics. Yet in the event they did not. The numerical collapse of trade union membership, the determined counterattack by elite parties on either side of the sectarian divide and the removal of key players from the leadership of the North's trade union movement in 2000–2001 led to a type of devolved government that would prove incapable of developing that wider unity.

In Scotland the issues were indeed different. But despite some significant achievements, the new Scottish governments after 1999 did not address the basic issues of under-development, deindustrialisation and poverty facing the Scottish people. The resulting political polarisation was of a different kind, but was also one that largely submerged issues of class politics as defined by the leaders of the TGWU 30 years before. As Alex Kitson put it in 1974 when arguing for a Scottish parliament:

> We shall not build a socialist society simply by saying over and over that the purpose of the Labour Party is to bring about a fundamental and irreversible shift in the balance of power and wealth in favour of working people. That outcome can only be secured when we change the nature and form of society, extending the forms of government in a way that gives working people a fuller understanding of the true nature of power and a greater say in all affairs [...] to develop their strength and gain experience.[60]

Wales

At the inaugural conference of the Wales TUC held in March 1974, the first motion carried was 'to set up an elected Legislative Assembly for Wales' to deal with the many industrial and economic problems in Wales. The motion was proposed by the South Wales NUM, and seconded by the T&G (Wales).

The Wales TUC produced a document that outlined a structure for a Wales Assembly; it set out proposals for a federal structure with England, this was to ensure that it could paint the assembly as a federal endeavour not a call for independence. The regional newspaper the *Western Mail* made the point that 'without the creation of the Wales TUC it is doubtful [if devolution] would have got off the ground, and without its persistence and pressure, it is doubtful that the Assembly would have been created'.

The commitment by Labour to set up an assembly for Wales took a new turn in 1979, when it was announced, with no prior warning, that a referendum would be held to determine the wishes of the people of

60 *Highway*, August 1974 (British Library).

Wales. The trade unions were incandescent; they believed it was a 'get out of jail card' or a 'Pontius Pilate' decision. The electorate of Wales, or those who bothered to vote, rejected the proposal by a landslide. George Wright, the T&G Wales Regional Secretary, described the campaign for the assembly as a 'shambles' and, in his opinion, 'the Labour Party staff went on holiday'.

It would be another 18 years before the proposition would again be put to the Welsh people. By 1997 there was a growing feeling that Wales needed to take back some control over its own affairs. A more determined effort was made to bring about a coalition of forces capable of building support for a transfer of powers from Westminster. This included the leadership of three of Wales' main political parties, Labour, Plaid Cymru and the Liberal Democrats. Only the governing Conservative Party remained adamantly opposed, but its support in Wales had collapsed; whereas 14 Conservative MPs had been returned to parliament from Wales in 1983, by 1997 there were none.

The way back to devolution was initiated after the general election of 1992, which was again lost by Labour. At the Wales TUC Conference a motion was carried calling on the Wales TUC and the Campaign for a Welsh Assembly to work together to establish a constitutional convention, as had been proposed in Scotland. However, this move was not welcomed by the Welsh Labour Party (WLP), which moved to nullify the impact of the motion. This concluded with its Conference in 1993, which opposed forming links with any all-party bodies to campaign for devolution.

The WLP instead established its own policy commission on devolution that would take evidence from its own organisations, the CLPs, its affiliates, the unions, and any outside body that wished to submit evidence. The Wales TUC then agreed that it would submit evidence to the WLP's policy commission and not have further links with the Campaign for a Welsh Assembly and to withdraw from the Constitutional Convention Steering Committee. In so doing the WLP established that it would be the singular body for framing the terms of debate on devolution for the wider labour movement in Wales.

The unions secured three places on the Policy Commission, drawn from trade union members of the WLP Executive Committee (WLP EC): Jim Hancock from the T&G, Terry Thomas from the GMB and Brian Curtis from RMT. The Commission set itself a three-year programme of work; in year one to take evidence from internal Labour Party bodies and in years two and three to receive evidence from and to consult with other bodies in Wales. Although not formally part of the process, the Wales TUC was involved in meetings with the Policy Commission in the first year of the project.

At this point the unions remained as significant influencers within Labour Party circles, and the development of the work of the Policy Commission was not an exception:

Whether overt or covert, the trade unions, particularly the affiliated unions, had a major influence on the process. Two of the
largest affiliated unions, the T&G and Unison, were extremely
keen on devolution, and this was in large part due to the personali-
ties involved. The T&G was led throughout this period by George
Wright, who had been a key player in the devolution debate in the
1970s and he continued to be a strong supporter. Although Wright
was no longer a member of the WLP EC, the T&G's representatives on the Executive were also strong supporters of devolution.[61]

The Policy Commission reported with some equanimity that the proposed
Welsh Assembly should take over the functions and budget of the Welsh
Office, have responsibility for quangos in Wales and should adopt a local
government committee system not a parliamentary system; but there was
little agreement over election to the assembly and taxation and legislative
powers.

On the method of election to the assembly, the WLP started this
process with a policy of two members per constituency in a 76-member
chamber, based on the 38 Westminster constituencies, using first-past-
the-post, with a commitment that at least one woman to be elected in
each constituency. At the end, the Policy Commission merely offered up
three alternatives: first-past-the-post, the additional member system and
regional lists.

The unions' position was to support first-past-the-post as it was
most likely to deliver a majority Labour administration and, incidentally,
deliver gender equality. Shadow Secretary of State, Ron Davies, supported
proportional representation, because he believed that support for devolution was on knife edge and any system that delivered a more or less
guaranteed Labour majority would be rejected by the voters.

The issue was eventually decided by the almost casual intervention of
Labour leader Tony Blair '[who] was considered to be generally uninter-
ested in the policy process that was taking place inside the Wales Labour
Party, and although he would later declare his support for proportional
representation, this decision, it was argued, principally arose out of the
need for an easy concession to the Liberal Democrats whom he was
courting'.[62]

An alternative view of Blair's commitment to proportional representation is that Blair was not an enthusiastic devolutionist, and the promise to
Scotland and Wales was really an inheritance from his predecessor, John

61 M.S. Lang, 'The Labour Party, the Trade Unions and Devolution in Wales', PhD
thesis (Cardiff University, School of European Studies, 2006), p.158.
62 Lang, 'The Labour Party', p.163.

Smith. The voting system – the additional member system – was adopted to stop the Scottish nationalists from getting a majority!

On the question of taxation, the Wales TUC put forward a proposal that the assembly should levy a precept on council tax in Wales in the way that police authorities and, as it transpired, the Greater London Authority, are funded. However, there was no majority within the WLP to give the assembly tax-raising powers.

On the question of legislative powers, the unions were divided. In 1993 at the Wales Labour Conference the Fire Brigades Union (FBU) tabled a motion that included legislative powers for the assembly, but the central thrust of this approach was nullified by amendments from the T&G and GMB. The Wales TUC probably reflected the views of its larger affiliates, which were also affiliated to Labour, that the assembly should have only secondary legislative powers, legislating within a framework set by Westminster.

Immediately after the 1997 general election that had delivered a landslide for 'New' Labour under Blair's leadership the WLP moved straight into the referendum campaign. It established a Strategy Committee of nine, four of which were trade union members of the Executive Committee: Jim Hancock and Elizabeth Pleece from the T&G, Terry Thomas of the GMB and Alun Williams of USDAW.

But the fact remained that the majority of Labour-affiliated unions and the Wales TUC had not, through the 1990s envisaged or wanted a referendum but were obliged to by the Labour leadership, particularly as there was to be a referendum in Scotland to decide whether to establish a Scottish parliament.

The need for a referendum was questioned because the laws and rules (primary legislation) would still originate from the UK government in Westminster, and there would still be a Minister of State with responsibility for Wales in the UK Cabinet. The title 'assembly' in itself differentiated this primarily administrative role from the wider law-making powers that were conferred on the Scottish Parliament under the parallel devolution agreement for Scotland.

This difference was highlighted particularly by the funding of the 'yes' campaigns in Scotland and Wales. In Scotland, Trade Unions for Labour (TUFL), the affiliated unions' umbrella body, handed over a cheque for £250,000 for the 'yes' vote. In Wales TUFL handed over money only in the hundreds of pounds.

The Wales TUC produced its own materials advocating a 'yes' vote and took advertising space in newspapers in the run up to the referendum, but 'individual unions were generally inactive. The FBU had very little appetite to campaign as a union, and gave little support; the AEEU did not have a campaign at all and contributed neither financial nor organisational help to the WLP campaign. Some unions such as Unison, the T&G and GMB were more supportive. The 'Yes for Wales' campaign, which was left with an £8,000 debt, received £2,000 from the GMB and T&G to help pay this off.[63]

Once the referendum was won a new source of conflict and dissention opened up. This time over the selection of candidates. The first fault line was gender equality. The WLP still had a policy of fielding at least 50 per cent women candidates, but there was only to be one AM elected per constituency.

For the constituency, rather than list, candidates the only way to do this was to 'twin' similar constituencies and decreeing in advance that at least one CLP would have to choose a women candidate, the other CLP in the 'twin' was then able to select a man. Women-only shortlists had, for the time being, been suspended from being used by the party.

The T&G was opposed to 'twinning', but when the issue was discussed at the WLP Executive Committee one of the union's two representatives broke ranks and voted to support. At the 1998 WLP Conference the T&G was the only union to oppose 'twinning'; the WLP Executive Committee position to support 'twinning' was carried.

The second point of conflict was the proposal to assemble a list of approved candidates; CLPs would only be able to choose from this approved list. Of course at this time the 'New' Labour operation was running like a well-oiled machine in getting right-wing candidates selected across the UK to support the 'New' Labour project.

There was established a Selections Board of 20 to draw up the list of approved candidates; the WLP had five seats, three of which went to union members: Jim Hancock from the T&G, Terry Thomas from the GMB, who was elected Chair, and Jean Brody from Unison. Two further trade unionists came onto the board in separate capacities.

The work of the board was not without controversy. For example, Tyrone O'Sullivan, NUM Chair at Tower Colliery, the last deep mine in Wales now run as a workers' co-op, was not selected as a candidate. There was a 'general feeling by critics of both proposals [twinning and the approved list] that they were means by which Blairite candidates could be selected and left wing members of the Party in Wales could be prevented from being selected'.[64]

The final piece of the jigsaw to be put in place was who would be leader, either of the Labour Group in the Welsh Assembly or as First Secretary should Labour gain a majority. At the beginning of the process in 1997 it was envisaged that the assembly would really be a super county council and, as such, the leader would not be such a prestigious position. But, in line with Blairite thinking for local government favouring a 'strong leader' model, there was a developmental process at work that decided that

63 Lang, 'The Labour Party', p.184.
64 Lang, 'The Labour Party', p.189.

the assembly would be based on the Cabinet system. All of a sudden the role of leader attracted significantly more prestige.

In the early period Rhodri Morgan emerged as front runner to be leader. At the Labour Party Conference in 1997 Morgan apparently attracted a good deal of union support, including from Jim Hancock for the T&G. With the emergence of the Cabinet system Ron Davies, the Secretary of State for Wales in Westminster, became more attracted to the post. Early union support for Morgan faded and switched to Davies, mostly because he was perceived as being Tony Blair's candidate.

Following the example of Scotland, there was to be established a tripartite electoral college in Wales, made up of CLPs, MPs and affiliates. The affiliates would not be required to hold a OMOV ballot of their members to determine how their votes would be cast.

Davies won in the CLP section and in the MPs' section, where Morgan did particularly poorly. He also ran out as winner with the unions:

> He ... received support from the Fire Brigades Union and NGA [National Graphical Association], neither of which held an OMOV ballot ... Ron Davies, however, benefited to a far greater extent from the lack of OMOV ballots in the trade unions; for example, the AEEU Regional Political Committee decided to support Ron Davies for no other reason than he was the Secretary of State.[65]

Davies' tenure was short lived; after his 'moment of madness' on Clapham Common he resigned. Battle was joined again by Rhodri Morgan and the arch-Blairite Alun Michael. The franchise was extended in the MPs' section to include MEPs and assembly candidates and, although there was an obligation on the CLP section to be balloted by OMOV no such requirement was placed upon the unions:

> The three largest unions in Wales, AEEU, GMB and T&G did not hold an OMOV ballot, but all voted in favour of Michael. The next biggest union, Unison, did hold an OMOV ballot and came down in favour of Morgan, Michael did not win a single trade union OMOV ballot, whereas Morgan won the support of all of the unions that did hold an OMOV ballot.[66]

It was not expected that Labour would win many of the regional list seats in the assembly and it was widely believed that the lists had been packed with Blairites solely to vote for Michael in the leadership election. In the event Labour only won one list seat, the seat of Alun Michael.

65 Lang, 'The Labour Party', p.190.
66 Lang, 'The Labour Party', p.192.

However, it soon became clear that Michael, as head of a minority administration in the Welsh Assembly, could not easily command the loyalty of the Assembly Labour Group, all of which were constituency members. Michael, realising that the game was up, resigned from the assembly and headed back to Parliament in Westminster.

The Assembly Labour Group and the WLP Executive Committee on 9 February 2000 endorsed Rhodri Morgan as Acting First Secretary. When nominations were formally opened Rhodri Morgan was the singular candidate and was unanimously agreed by a joint meeting of the Assembly Labour Group and the WLP Executive Committee.

After almost three years, with many unions clearly held in the sway of the Labour leadership in London and two attempts by 'New' Labour to impose one of its own on Wales, a leader emerged commanding the support of all the Assembly and Executive members.

London – the Livingstone Years

In its 1997 general election manifesto Labour had made a promise to introduce devolution for Scotland and Wales, if endorsed by a referendum. It made a similar pledge for London, a restoration of regional government, if endorsed by a referendum of London voters. Ken Livingstone had maintained a high profile as a London MP during the later 1980s and 1990s and remained closely associated with the idea of London regional government so became an early front runner to become leader of any new political arrangement for London.

In London, the strong relationship between the T&G and Ken Livingstone went back a long way, back to the days of the GLC of the early 1980s. Then, the incoming Labour administration had published a voluminous *London Plan*, included in which were plans to strategically intervene in the London economy, particularly to protect London's manufacturing base. Some of these economic initiatives were to be led by the Popular Planning Unit, part of the GLC; the strategic intervention in the London economy was to be carried out by a new arm's length body, the Greater London Enterprise Board (GLEB).

Barry Camfield was then the Regional Education Officer and an early supporter of these new initiatives. He deployed his team of trade union studies tutors to work with shop stewards and workers' reps in firms and sectors that were being promoted by the Popular Planning Unit or in which GLEB was taking a stake. A seat on the GLEB was held by the T&G Regional Secretary, Sid Staden; upon Staden's retirement this seat was taken by Camfield.

Camfield and Livingstone remained close when Livingstone, after the GLC was abolished by Margaret Thatcher, became an MP in Brent, in northwest London. As Regional Secretary in the late 1990s, Camfield was able to mobilise Region 1 of the union to support Livingstone in his bid to become Labour's candidate to be Mayor of London, the Blairite settlement for reinstated regional government. It is true that the T&G, like Livingstone himself, originally opposed the idea of devolution with an executive mayor, favouring a return to a GLC local government model.

In supporting Livingstone, Camfield was opposed by Bill Morris, who wanted the union to support Blair's candidate, Frank Dobson. There was a showdown between the two at the London Labour Party Conference at Hammersmith Town Hall, resulting in a breach that was never to heal; Morris pledged his support to Assistant General Secretary and former Scottish Regional Secretary, Jimmy Elsby, to succeed Margaret Prosser as Deputy General Secretary on her retirement. The election was won by Tony Woodley.

In Ken Livingstone's memoirs one passage particularly reflects the fevered atmosphere of the time:

> [T]he left usually opposed unions being forced to ballot because it helped the right, but now the positions were reversed, with Blair supporting a trade union fix and the left demanding ballots. The key would be if, after all their years of opposition to ending the block voting system, the London region Transport and General decided to ballot. Simon [Fletcher] and I had a rare disagreement when I jumped the gun in favour of balloting whereas he wanted to wait until the London region of the T&G met the next day. Barry Camfield, the London T&G organiser, let me address their committee and asked me to wait outside 'for a few minutes'. After an hour of heated debate I was told they would call a ballot. I went on to win by 85.8 per cent to Glenda's [Jackson] 7.3 and Frank's 6.9. When the T&G conveyed the news to Downing Street the response was, I'm told, 'Fuck. Who was second?' 'Glenda'. 'Fuck'. 'Dobbo's third'. 'Oh, God'.[67]

When it was clear that Livingstone would not be adopted as Labour candidate because of his refusal to accept the private public partnership on the underground Camfield was against Livingstone breaking ranks to stand as an independent. Your present author, then the Region 1 Policy Officer, was dispatched to meet Livingstone's political advisor, Simon Fletcher, in a pub near Congress House to pass on Camfield's message. Region 1 did get its political fund donation to Livingstone just in time, before Livingstone announced he was standing as an independent and was expelled from the Labour Party. Fletcher has subsequently made the point that, although Livingstone accepted that his expulsion would be almost immediate, he most certainly did not want any union disaffiliated for officially supporting him once he was outside the party.

---

67 Livingstone, *You Can't Say That*, p.395.

Early in 2000 Camfield was appointed Assistant General Secretary and moved to head office. He was replaced by Eddie McDermott, a surprise appointment, as McDermott had not previously been identified with the broad left tradition in Region 1.

For his first term, Mayor Livingstone sat as an Independent and only latterly was readmitted to Labour to contest the election for his second term as Labour's candidate. Nonetheless, the T&G in London was immersed in City Hall politics from 2000 to 2008. The union was an active participant in the annual Respect, later renamed Rise, anti-racist festival. The T&G was a major funder of, and a key participant in, the Third European Social Forum, the anti-globalisation event closely identified with Livingstone's mayoralty held at Alexandra Palace in October 2004.

However, the T&G made no progress on its central industrial demand on Livingstone that Transport for London (T/L) should act as a collective bargaining forum, holding the ring between the private bus operators on the one hand and the union on the other, with the intention of negotiating a common pay rate across London's buses rather than separate terms and conditions in each of the private bus companies. If there was to be tendering for routes the union wanted wages taken out of the equation so that companies tendered on the basis of quality of service and did not undercut each other by paying lower wages.

This lack of progress is all the more of a mystery as Livingstone had created three places on the T/L board that were filled by nominees from ASLEF (the Associated Society of Locomotive Engineers and Firemen, representing underground train drivers), RMT (tube train drivers and underground staff) and the T&G (London's buses). The T&G was represented initially by its lead London Bus Officer, Ollie Jackson, and latterly by Regional Organiser Pat O'Keeffe, who had a background in civil aviation at Heathrow. RMT had earlier withdrawn from the T/L board, but in any event all three posts were abolished when Boris Johnson succeeded Livingstone as London Mayor in 2008. When Sadiq Khan won back the mayoralty for Labour in 2016, he recreated just one seat on the T/L Board for the unions, allocated to the TUC's London, Eastern & South East Region, thus not restoring a direct link between London's transport unions and the board.

In the early 2000s Livingstone won for London the right to stage the Olympic Games in 2008; the primary purpose of which was to enable a major redevelopment of the lower Lea valley in London's more or less derelict docklands on the north bank of the Thames. There was to be a trade union seat on the board of the organisation charged with overseeing the huge construction project of building the new stadia and Olympic village, the Olympic Delivery Authority (ODA). This seat was not in Livingstone's gift but was appointed by the responsible government minster, Tessa Jowell MP. Although McDermott had made it very clear that he wanted the seat appointed at regional level, and that he should be appointed, there was a general view among the unions, including the TUC, that a regional appointment would be inappropriate. So, even though he had moved on to national responsibilities, Barry Camfield found himself with a renewed London mandate when he was appointed to the ODA board.

During the Livingstone era the dreadful bomb attacks on the London Underground and a bus took place on 7 July 2005, causing 52 passenger fatalities. There were further attempted bombings a fortnight later on 21 July on the underground and a bus – just the detonators exploded, with no fatalities. Ken Livingstone was widely credited with great political acumen in his response to the bombings, promoting the idea of a united London and ensuring that an anti-Muslim narrative did not develop as part of the public discourse.

The drivers of the two buses targeted in the attacks on the 7 and 21 July, George Psaradakis and Mark Maybanks, both coincidentally from Stratford garage, were held to have conducted themselves in an exemplary fashion; the GEC awarded the pair the union's Gold Medal. The medals were presented by the Chancellor of the Exchequer, and T&G member, Gordon Brown MP at a ceremony at Transport House in May 2006.[68]

The T&G, now part of Unite, maintained its relationship with Livingstone, again supporting him as Labour's candidate for the 2012 mayoral election, in which Johnson won for a further four-year term. This defeat marked the effective retirement of Livingstone from front line politics.

The English Regions

John Smith's pledge to the 35th BDC in 1993 did not stand the test of time so far as England was concerned. Labour's proposals for the English regions, excluding London, were much more modest. There was an ill-fated referendum to test whether a regional assembly should be established in the North East, but Labour's principal vehicle for regional devolution in England, excluding London, which had an executive mayor with economic development as part of the portfolio, was to be a half-way house – unelected regional development agencies based on the newly defined government office regions.

As has been noted previously, the T&G regional boundaries were very idiosyncratic, Region 1 had within its borders about half the geographic area of the government's new South East Region. In the late 1990s Region 1 Regional Secretary Barry Camfield was appointed to the board of SEEDA (South East England Development Agency), in which role he pressed for union organisation and recognition where the agency may have had dealings with non-union firms and for industrial democracy where the agency linked up with firms that had union recognition.

68 http://news.bbc.co.uk/1/hi/england/london/4759777.stm.

The regional development agencies, with no elected members (although being an elected body offers no protection from a determined Conservative government, as the Livingstone-led GLC discovered in the 1980s), became an early casualty of the austerity measures introduced by the Conservative-led coalition in 2010, when they were unceremoniously abolished.

International

While Ron Todd was closely identified with the anti-apartheid struggle in South Africa, Bill Morris took few publicised initiatives in international affairs, although, indicative of his Christian belief, he did take an interest in Haiti and the work of priest and politician Jean-Bertrand Aristide. Industrial work with the international union federations ITSs (international trade secretariats), subsequently rebranded GUFs (global union federations)) was, by and large, handled by the appropriate Trade Group National Secretary.

When Barry Camfield was appointed Assistant General Secretary in 2000 with responsibility for international solidarity he determined that the union should no longer have an *ad hoc* or scattergun approach to international solidarity work but instead should focus on key areas – Cuba, Palestine and Colombia. Bolivarian Venezuela, under Hugo Chávez, was soon added to the list.

Movement on Palestine and Cuba coincided with Tony Woodley's election as General Secretary of the T&G in May 2003. The union made an intervention in support of Palestine at the TUC Congress and, more famously, campaigned in support of Cuban or Miami 5.

Palestine
The T&G had been gradually developing policy on Palestine. The 36th BDC (1995) carried a motion discussing the expanding Israeli settlements in the Occupied Palestinian Territories:

> This is a deliberate plan to annex part of the occupied territories and prevent a viable Palestinian state being established. Conference call on the GEC to use its influence in the international workers' movement to press for the cancellation of all Israeli settlement activity and the evacuation of all Israeli settlements in the occupied territories including those in the West Bank, Gaza Strip and East Jerusalem.[69]

---

69 Minutes of the Proceedings of the 36th Biennial Delegate Conference 1995, p.106.

The union did not return to the issue of Palestine again until the 39th BDC (2001). First, at the conference the Frank Cousins Peace Prize was awarded posthumously to the late Dr Yousef Allan, the representative in Britain of the Palestine General Federation of Trade Unions and the Delegate General of Palestine to Ireland. The minutes record: 'His energy and personal commitment to his nation's struggle for liberation made a profound impact on the political establishment in both countries'.[70]

Second, a more comprehensive motion was carried calling for an end to settlements, the right of return for Palestinian refugees, the establishment of a Palestinian state and strengthened relations between the T&G and Palestinian unions and women's groups.

Replying to the debate, Deputy General Secretary Margaret Prosser somewhat disingenuously, particularly in the context of the motion, said that 'the T&G had good relations with Histradut, the union that represents Israeli workers'. She went on to say 'the Israeli Government ... do not ... want matters to be settled. As fast as they reach an agreement with the Palestine Liberation Organisation, then they move the goalposts and ask for something further'.[71]

The pace of support for Palestine certainly quickened during the 2000s. At the 40th BDC (2003) the Frank Cousins Peace Prize was awarded to Belinda Coote, Chief Executive of Medical Aid for Palestinians, and a further comprehensive motion was carried, as happened again at the 41st BDC (2005).

The TUC Congress in 2006 was a watershed in breaking the log-jam of even-handedness that Congress House had traditionally displayed when dealing with Israel and Palestine. A composite motion at the Congress to be moved by the FBU aimed to break with that policy, to commit the TUC to be explicitly supportive of the Palestinian cause, the Palestine General Federation of Trade Unions and the Palestine Solidarity Campaign.

As Congress broke up at the close of business with the General Council's position still unclear, Tony Woodley held the T&G delegation back and, when the hall was empty of other delegates, no doubt buoyed by the union's evolving policy of support for Palestine, he made an impassioned plea for the T&G to back the composite motion to commit the TUC to support Palestinian rights and the Palestinian cause.

The following day, after a long debate that included speakers from a wide range of unions, and eventually a General Council recommendation to support, a recommendation that would not have been made if not for a long campaign by affiliates led particularly by the FBU, the composite was carried. Truly a watershed moment.

70 Minutes of the Proceedings of the 39th Biennial Delegate Conference 2001.
71 Minutes of the Proceedings of the 39th Biennial Delegate Conference 2001.

Unite remains an important affiliate of the Palestine Solidarity Campaign and the Labour Palestine campaign.

War in Iraq

Following on from the first Gulf War of 1990–1991, a US-led response to the Iraqi invasion of Kuwait, the victorious Western coalition imposed harsh economic sanctions against Iraq. These sanctions were said to be imposed partly because Iraq was not in compliance with the terms of ending the war, that it divest itself of all weapons of mass destruction – nuclear, biological and chemical.

The sanctions clearly had a devastating impact on the general population of Iraq, as noted almost a decade later by the 38th BDC held in 1999: 'On Iraq, the General Executive Council reiterates the sentiments expressed to the Prime Minister last year, which called for further diplomatic efforts to be made to find a permanent and peaceful solution, including the ending of economic sanctions, which are causing further deprivation and hardship to the innocent people of Iraq'.[72] In the light of his subsequent actions in leading Britain, as junior partner to the US, into the second war against Iraq in the early 2000s, it has to be questioned if the Prime Minister was serious or sincere in the way that the GEC may have thought.

It was in the aftermath of 9/11 that the Stop the War Coalition was founded in September 2001, with a particular mission to campaign against the likely retaliatory war to be launched by the US and, as a concomitant, to campaign against any escalation to something worse than the 11 September atrocity taking place.

Most left of centre campaigns would seek to involve the unions for reasons of organisational and financial support and for links with organised, and likely politically committed, workers. It was not at all clear that the unions, including the T&G, were completely on board with the new campaign, at least in the early phase. This reluctance may have been to avoid falling further out of favour with the Labour Party leadership:

> Initially ... trade union support for the Stop the War Coalition was pretty thin. ASLEF, the train drivers' union, was strongly supportive from the start under Mick Rix's leadership, as was NATFHE, the lecturers' union, and its general secretary, Paul Mackney. The RMT's Bob Crow was an early stalwart. The largest unions – Unison, Amicus [then the AEEU and MSF in the process of merging], the T&G and the GMB – held aloof initially, as did the TUC itself.[73]

---

72   Minutes of the Proceedings of the 38th Biennial Delegate Conference 1999, p.92.
73   A. Murray & L. German, *Stop the War: the Story of Britain's Biggest Mass Movement* (Bookmarks, 2005), p.55.

An anti-war rally was held in Hyde Park on 28 September 2002, addressed by, among others, Barry Camfield, the T&G's Assistant General Secretary, dubbed by Andrew Murray in interview as 'a consistent anti-war campaigner'.

By the time that the Stop the War Coalition mobilised the largest demonstration ever seen in Britain on 15 February 2003, two million people demonstrating against the impending war in Iraq, many of the unions had been won over, with their leaders, including the T&G's, speaking that day: 'the trade union movement was more than well represented in London. Tony Woodley of the T&G, Paul Mackney of NATFHE, Mark Serwotka of the civil servants' PCS, Mick Rix from ASLEF, Billy Hayes from the Communication Workers' Union and the RMT's Bob Crow all made powerful speeches'.[74]

With no evidence of any link between al-Qaeda and Saddam Hussein's Iraq, the US falsely made the link – coupled with the false assertion that Iraq was in possession of weapons of mass destruction – and so launched a new war against Iraq in March 2003.

At the 40th BDC, held after the 2003 mass demonstration, the narrative of Composite 30 on Iraq hit all the right buttons – no link between al-Qaeda and the Iraqi regime; a real link between those driving for regime change and US petrochemical interests; explicit condemnation of the US and Britain for the military attack on Iraq. The composite motion resolved to 'identify the T&G more closely with the Stop the War Coalition'.[75]

The closer identification by many unions with the Stop the War Coalition was almost shattered in the Autumn of 2004 with unions supporting two opposing positions on what was now the occupation of Iraq at the TUC Congress and then a fortnight later at the Labour Party Conference. The motion carried at Congress was helpful. The motion carried at Conference was most unhelpful, other than to the Labour Party leadership war party. But a potential crisis was averted – no union broke ranks. Murray and German quote Tony Woodley on this issue:

> The anti-war movement is one of the remarkable achievements of our time. Its breadth, strength and unity have helped reinvigorate progressive politics in Britain. That has not been without complications. But I am proud of the part trade unions have played in Stop the War Coalition ... Certainly, now is not the time for splits or resignations. It is time for unity against the war danger, and unity to get the most rapid withdrawal from Iraq. For me it is quite

74 Murray & German, *Stop the War*, p.159.
75 Minutes of the Proceedings of the 40th Biennial Delegate Conference 2003, p.64.

simple. We cannot have progress without peace. We will not have peace without a powerful peace movement. Let's stick together.[76]

Throughout this period Andrew Murray, initially working for ASLEF and latterly the T&G, was the lynchpin in linking the trade unions with the anti-war movement. Unite remains an important affiliate of the Stop the War Coalition.

Cuba and the Miami 5
Although it would become a major international campaigning issue for the left (and turned into a feature film starring Penélope Cruz) the cause of the Miami 5 (five Cuban intelligence agents infiltrated into the US to fight Miami-based Cuban counter-revolutionaries and terrorists, who were captured by the FBI and sentenced to excessively long prison terms, including in some cases double life) had a very quiet, if hardly noticed, introduction to the T&G.

A guest at the 39th BDC (2001) Fernando Pérez Concepión, Secretary of the Cuban transport workers' union, spoke about the Miami 5 in his speech to Conference. The minutes record:

[H]e drew attention to the plight of the five Cuban people who had been in prison for 17 months in America. The only crime they have committed he said was protecting their country from the Mafia Cubana in America, in their plans to sabotage their way of life and prosperity through their inhuman actions like the blockade. Bro Pérez Concepión asked delegates to press for their urgent release and expressed the belief that with labour movement solidarity this goal could be achieved.[77]

The Cuba Solidarity Campaign had brought Olga Salanueva, wife of René González, one of the Miami 5, to London in the Autumn 2002 to meet Amnesty International; CSC (the Cuba Solidarity Campaign) had organised a speaking tour of Britain by the Miami 5's lawyer earlier that year. In 2005, the Cuba Solidarity Campaign again organised a speaking tour for Olga Salanueva, which included a breakfast meeting for trade union leaders held in the Council Chamber of Transport House, hosted by Assistant General Secretary, Barry Camfield.

Although Tony Woodley spoke at the CSC fringe meeting at the union's conference in 2007, it was not until 2008 that he picked up campaigning in

76 Murray & German, *Stop the War*, p.263.
77 Manuscript of Minutes of the Proceedings of the 39th Biennial Delegate Conference 2001, p.96.

Figure 5: Assistant General Secretary, Len McCluskey, Director of the Cuba Solidarity Campaign, Rob Miller, and officers of the United Steel Workers at the US Embassy in London lobbying on behalf of the Miami 5, 2008

earnest. Woodley went to Havana for the May Day celebrations in 2008. While there, he met with the President of the National Assembly, Ricardo Alarcón; but of equal importance for future campaigning, he met the wives of some of the Miami 5. The key moment of the meeting with the wives was when Woodley asked Adriana Perez, wife of Gerardo Hernández, what she missed most. Adriana replied it was going into the kitchen each morning and seeing the empty places where their kids would have sat had Gerardo not been in jail; the children she would never have. Everyone at the meeting was reduced to tears and Woodley resolved that the T&G would join the campaign – firstly for visitation rights for family members which had mainly been denied by the US authorities and subsequently for freedom for the Miami 5.

Upon Woodley's return to London, campaign activity was stepped up. A meeting involving Woodley, TUC General Secretary Brendan Barber and Unison General Secretary Dave Prentis was arranged with David Miliband, then Foreign Secretary in Gordon Brown's government, who very reluctantly wrote a letter about the Miami 5 to Condoleezza Rice, his opposite number in the US government. Woodley also got in touch with Andy Stern of the SEIU, getting him to write to President Bush asking for visas for the wives.

When, under the Obama presidency, Hillary Clinton, then US Secretary of State, came to London Woodley arranged that Brown would hand her a letter about visitation rights. As WikiLeaks subsequently showed, this latter action caused a minor panic in the US embassy. The actions of that year peaked at Labour Party Conference, with a carefully choreographed meeting between Adriana and Olga and Gordon Brown, seemingly a chance encounter as he was going into the Unite/T&G reception.

In 2009 Len McCluskey and Brendan Barber went to Havana for the May Day celebrations and the solidarity conference held the following day. The following year, acting on a direct request from Woodley to get involved with the campaign, the SEIU and the United Steel Workers (a US general union with which Unite subsequently formed a strategic partnership, Workers Uniting) went to Havana for the May Day rally and the solidarity conference. Woodley also arranged for the Teamsters to write to the US Department of Homeland Security, asking for Olga to be allowed to visit René. Tony Woodley frequently travelled to the US to visit Gerardo and the others in prison.

Tony retired as General Secretary as the T&G transformed itself into Unite. The new union kept up the campaign under Len McCluskey's leadership until the Miami 5 were eventually released, albeit in stages: René in 2011, Fernando González in February 2014, with the remaining three Gerardo, Ramón Labañino and Antonio Guerrero, as part of the re-establishment of diplomatic relations between the US and Cuba, in December 2014.

Unite has remained an important affiliate of the Cuba Solidarity Campaign and other Latin American solidarity groups, including Justice for Colombia, Venezuela Solidarity Campaign, Brazil Solidarity Initiative and Nicaragua Solidarity Campaign.

Summary

It would have to be said that for the T&G it was a lean time in its relations with Labour, both as a party and in government during the 1990s and into the twenty-first century. As far as the party was concerned, the union was always fighting a rearguard action to remain as an affiliated organisation; attempts were made to exclude the affiliated unions from participation in the selection of the leader and parliamentary candidates, although at the end of this period the union-supported Ed Miliband did become party leader. Blair and his circle would have preferred to end the formal relationship with the unions.

In government, Labour made few concessions on workplace legislation. Either by personal inclination or ideological commitment, Blair was immovable on this issue. The National Minimum Wage, restoration of union rights at GCHQ, an inadequate new statutory recognition procedure and the right to be accompanied at grievance or disciplinary hearings were no substitute for the repeal of the Tory anti-union laws.

As is usual, Labour in government remained in lock step with the US over foreign policy. So although the union won some minor concessions with the Miami 5 campaign, on the big foreign policy issue, war in Iraq, the T&G, like all other social movements, was completely and utterly ignored.

6

Towards Unite – a New Type of Union

Although the T&G had grown in most part by organising in the rapidly expanding labour market of the post-war period, it had also grown by merger, with many smaller unions transferring their engagements to the T&G. In this chapter we look at how the merger strategy had stalled by the start of the 1990s; at how the natural fit of a merger with the GMB came to nothing, and then the perhaps an unlikely merger with Amicus came about to form Unite.

Merger with T&G Not Favourable

There had been no sizable transfers of engagements to the T&G since the Agricultural Workers and the Textile Workers in the early 1980s, and this was indicative that there was a problem with this part of any growth strategy. This problem was amplified in 1990 when the National Union of Seamen (NUS) opted to merge with the National Union of Railwaymen (NUR) to form the RMT, rather than transfer its engagements to the T&G.

There are both organisational and personal issues to be resolved with any trade union merger. The merger of a smaller union into a larger union will invariably be carried out by transfer of engagements, where the smaller union will usually become just one of any number of sections in the larger union and the general secretary may find themselves just one of a number of second-ranking full-time officials. An amalgamation of two mid-sized unions, such as the NUS and NUR, at least gives a chance of equity in organisational structure, important for lay activists and the positioning of officials.

The T&G and GMB

The 35th BDC (1993) tried to grasp this nettle with support for what would have been a full-blown amalgamation, not a transfer of engagements, with the GMB. Composite Motion 45 concluded: 'Conference instructs the GEC and Executive Officers to continue to promote closer working relations with the GMB, with a view to a merger at some time in the future. We should pursue a programme of meaningful dialogue, with a view to developing a positive partnership leading towards a merger'.[1]

By the time of the 36th BDC in 1995 it was clear that the anticipated merger with the GMB was not proceeding at all well, if at all. Composite Motion 48 acknowledged the apparent cooling in relations: 'Conference views with deep regret the missed opportunity of pursuing a speedy and effective merger of the two unions in the certainty that the combined strength of a 1.5 million plus general workers' union would be a powerful force for change in British society'. At the same Conference Motion 394 was carried, calling for a transfer of engagements by the NUM to the T&G.

Replying to the debate, Bill Morris welcomed the transfer of the Electrical & Plumbing Industries Union (EPIU) into the T&G, but as far as the GMB was concerned he is recorded as declaring that 'he had been disappointed when [t]he GMB conference felt unable to proceed with the formal talks'. With regard to the NUM, a union that few believed that he would welcome into the T&G, he is recorded as drawing attention to 'the federation type structure of the NUM which would mean that that union had to amalgamate itself before any transfer of engagement could take place'.[2]

At the 37th BDC (1997) Composite Motion 52 'welcomes recent mergers into the union, instructs the General Executive Council to seek mergers with other unions, and build upon BDC policy adopted in 1995 to promote the concept of a new union based on industrial logic'.[3] At the same conference videos were played bringing greetings from John Edmonds, General Secretary of the GMB and George Brumwell, General Secretary of UCATT (Union of Construction, Allied Trades and Technicians). This was perhaps indicative that the GMB merger had not quite expired and that a transfer of engagements by the construction workers' union was a possibility. Indeed, the minutes record Margaret Prosser replying to the debate:

1 Minutes of the Proceedings of the 35th Biennial Delegate Conference 1993, pp.8–9.

2 Minutes of the Proceedings of the 36th Biennial Delegate Conference 1995, pp.54–55.

3 Minutes of the Proceedings of the 37th Biennial Delegate Conference 1997, pp.34–35.

[T]he T&G continued to pursue a strategy of looking at closer working relationships with for example the GMB and she welcomed the National Association of Licenced House Managers who had recently voted to join the T&G. Sister Prosser reported that the policy agreed at the previous BDC with regard to closer working relationships with the GMB continued to be pursued and that developments in the construction industry were kept under scrutiny.[4]

But merger with the GMB remained elusive, and negotiations with UCATT came to nothing. At the same time, there was a point of view gaining currency that the GMB was able to pursue a more successful strategic approach in persuading smaller unions to transfer their engagements to it. In the period since the textile workers and the agricultural workers had transferred to the T&G, the GMB had managed to swallow up a number of small and medium-sized textile workers' unions, including the National Union of Tailors & Garment Workers, even though the largest union in the sector had become part of the T&G. In addition, it had attracted a number of other, mainly white-collar, small unions to its fold.

The GMB also captured the Furniture, Timber and Allied Trades Union (FTAT). The 'loss' of FTAT was felt particularly strongly by the T&G broad left as it was believed that there was great affinity between the left in the two unions, an affinity that should have delivered a result for the T&G.

By the time of the 38th BDC (1999), any discussion about merger with the GMB had dropped off the agenda, as indeed had any discussion of a general merger strategy. Composite Motion 5, entitled 'A Stronger T&G', dealt exclusively with recruitment and organising, focusing particularly on the construction industry and young workers.

The T&G and Amicus, and Possibly the GMB

There was to be a passage of 20 years before anything as bold as merger with the GMB would be put before the T&G's membership again – except this time it was the mega-merger with Amicus, a merger that created Unite. A transfer of engagements by the construction workers' union UCATT had to also wait until well into the days of this new union.

With the union's base in manufacturing now seriously in decline, a serious strategic move needed to be considered. Overall, T&G membership was in decline, by the equivalent of a trade group every five or six years (Table 3):

---

4 Minutes of the Proceedings of the 37th Biennial Delegate Conference 1997, p.39.

Table 3: T&G Membership Numbers

Year	Numbers
2000–2001	858,804
2001–2002	848,809
2002–2003	835,351
2003–2004	816,986
2004–2005	806,938
2005–2006	777,325
2006–2007	761,336
Net loss	97,468

Source: *Annual Reports*, Certification Officer.

In interview, Len McCluskey recalled that initially a merger with Amicus was not something that was seriously contemplated, although the election of Derek Simpson as Amicus General Secretary was encouraging. One of Simpson's first acts was to repudiate a no-strike deal with EasyJet, which allowed the T&G to sign a proper recognition agreement with the airline. Murray quotes perhaps a very prescient Jack Jones: 'Simpson must be cultivated; he can be a good friend'.[5]

Prior to Simpson's election, Amicus, or its core predecessor the AEEU, had been hoovering up all sorts of mid-sized and small unions and professional associations. The T&G had tried to win the print workers' union GPMU (Graphical, Paper & Media Union), but had lost out to Amicus.

McCluskey recalls that he suggested to Tony Woodley that the T&G should try to revive merger talks with the GMB. Woodley had recently been to China with the GMB General Secretary Kevin Curran, where they had formed a close working relationship. When Simpson discovered that these talks were taking place he approached Woodley and demanded that Amicus be included in a three-way mega-merger.

The idea of a three-way merger was put to and endorsed by the GEC at a special meeting held in February 2005, although it was clear that Amicus seemed keener to get the process started than the GMB. General Secretary Tony Woodley's report to the Council noted that 'the talks to create this New Union will, we hope, be with Amicus and the GMB simultaneously, but in any case, we will start with Amicus'.[6]

Following endorsement of Woodley's report the Council then agreed that 'similar letters from both unions will go to the General Secretary of the GMB, Kevin Curran, inviting them to join negotiations as an equal

5 Murray, *New Labour Nightmare*, p.35.
6 General Executive Council Minutes, February 2005, p.2.

partner to create this new giant union'.[7] But Kevin Curran was soon replaced by Paul Kenny as GMB General Secretary; Kenny most certainly was not keen on the mega-merger. In December 2006, the recalled 41st BDC was asked to consider proceeding to a ballot of the membership on a merger involving just the T&G and Amicus.

For the T&G Woodley had argued at the original 41st BDC in 2005 that the merger would be based on three essential principles: inviolable lay democracy, organising and equalities.[8] These were themes that he returned to at the recalled BDC 17 months later in December 2006, clearly satisfied that these principles had been upheld in the merger negotiations.[9]

Andrew Murray recalled in interview that the merger process was not without controversy within the union. Region 6 saw Amicus as being particularly short on lay democracy; Region 1 was very concerned about the right-wing tradition within Amicus; and Diana Holland, then National Officer for Women & Equalities, was said to be concerned that there was little commitment to equalities within Amicus – not least she was concerned that the hard-won designated seats for women and ethnic minority members on the union's committees and conferences could soon disappear. Among the T&G leadership group there was anxiety because the T&G had only recently been won back from the drift to the right under Bill Morris, but in Amicus there was scant tradition of left organisation in the modern union, although of course its component parts had very proud and serious histories going back over 100 years – highlighting particularly such luminaries from Tom Mann through to Hugh Scanlon.

Winning Unite as a Union of the Left

In interview, Len McCluskey recalled that he was confident that the T&G culture of a 'fighting back' union would win through; he believed that the Amicus negotiators agreed to almost anything in the merger talks because they thought they would win control of the new union and would scrap anything they did not like.

Once the Unite merger was formalised, like Morris and Edmunds in the previous era, the differences between Woodley and Derek Simpson came increasingly to the surface. So much so that at one point, according to McCluskey in interview, Woodley consulted a QC about unpicking the merger.

A further example of this frosty relationship emerged on vesting day. Unite was officially launched on 1 May 2007. Ken Livingstone had agreed

7 General Executive Council Minutes, February 2005, p.2.
8 Minutes of the Proceedings of the 41st Biennial Delegate Conference 2005, p.32.
9 Minutes of the Proceedings of the Recalled 41st Biennial Delegate Conference 2006, pp.21–22.

that the launch would be the theme of his annual May Day reception for trade unionists held at City Hall. Simpson, taking offence – either real or contrived – because Woodley had appeared on the radio that morning, failed to appear at the reception, an event to mark the creation of a new union of which he was the joint leader.

The unofficial aspects of the two unions, particularly the left organisation of shop stewards and branch activists, were slow to reflect the official merger. An important gesture of confidence was the agreement, at a meeting in Birmingham of over 200 activists on 21 February 2009, for the T&G Broad Left and Amicus Unity Gazette to merge into a single left grouping, United Left.

By 2010, it could be said that the project to create Unite, as a new type of union, had been completed. With a new single General Secretary in Len McCluskey, committed to the Woodley era ethos of being an organising union, Unite would need to weld together all the disparate parts. A question for the future may be how far engagement in communities and involvement in national political campaigns can create a new mass base for trade union organisation.

Index